# WHERE'S MY LEMONADE?

17 Inspirational Stories to Keep You Going When Life Gives You Lemons.

Compiled by

## Jamie Brockhurst and Raeesa Mumith

# DEDICATION

This book is dedicated to the Mental Health Foundation, whose work we admire and support with the profits of this book. This book is also dedicated to anyone who has ever struggled with their mental well-being, there is always a light at the end of the tunnel, keep going.

'Prevention is at the heart of what we do, because the best way to deal with a crisis is to prevent it from happening in the first place.'

-The Mental Health Foundation

# COPYRIGHT AND DISCLAIMERS

# Contents

# INTRODUCTION

Just like physical health, mental health can and will fluctuate throughout our lifetime. Sometimes we are doing great, confidence is high, fulfillment is flowing and we have that wonderful feeling of peace within us.

Sometimes however, it can feel as though we are fumbling our way through life - overwhelmed by the responsibilities and challenges and trying to crawl through the storm.

The truth is, life can and will throw lemons at us.

Big yellow curve balls that challenge us to our limits, test our resilience and make it hard to keep our head above water. No one is immune to life's lemons, we will all face our own challenges along the way and it is our mental health that takes the brunt of it. So what can we do about it?

It's been said:

"When life gives you lemons, make lemonade."

Which is all good and well. But as you're riding the storm you find yourself asking in an exhausted, frustrated and burnt out state.... **"Where the $@*!*% is my lemonade?!"**.

This book is dedicated to reminding you that there is always lemonade after the lemons.

No matter where you are currently, how deep you are in the dark or how much you are suffering right now, there is always hope. This book is dedicated to reminding you that there is always a light at the end of the tunnel, and that you will one day reach it - no matter how dark it gets on the way.

Life does get better, it does get easier and you will be happy.

We know this because we have been there too. Both of us have felt riddled with anxiety, poor mental health and hopelessness, as though we were stuck in the dark place and that the struggle was too much. We lacked confidence, calmness and peace and didn't know if that would ever change. But guess what, it did, it really, really did. Life is so very different, better than either of us previously could have imagined.

We want this for you too. We want you to feel like you again. We want to restore your hope, your happiness and your inner peace, just like we have experienced ourselves.

So we asked 17 people what their secret to happiness and contentment was, we asked them how they managed their challenges with their mental health. To follow the analogy, we asked them how they made lemonade out of lemons.

What you'll find in this book are those stories.

Our incredible authors share stories of building body confidence and self love. Tales of resilience, courage and authenticity. We talk about gratitude, the importance of play (yes even as adults) and talk frankly and honestly about mental obstacles.

These stories are real, and maybe not too dissimilar form your own. Each person has their own story of struggle, but they made it through and these are the stories about how they did it against the odds.

It's the secret to how they made their lemonade.

Think of each individual chapter as a small nugget of inspiration. They're meant to be dipped into as and when you need them to offer insights, ideas, tips and tricks to help you conquer.

A little about us…

We are Jamie and Raeesa, two twenty-something friends who have come together with the single purpose of helping you start to feel like you again.

Writing this book has been a passion project and every penny of profit is being donated to the Mental Health Foundation. We hope to raise money for this charity to help those struggling with their mental wellbeing- help someone by helping yourself.

With love,

Jamie and Raeesa

Website: www.wheresmylemonade.com

Email: wheresmylemonade@gmail.com

# CHAPTER 1

# ACCEPTANCE WAS THE KEY

## By Tulsi

My name is Tulsi, I am an inspirational speaker specialised in self-worth, confidence and practising authenticity. My passion for helping people derives from my experiences and I want to help people manifest their true potential.

I fell into being a speaker purely by chance. Looking back, it was a clear sign that I needed to share my story to help others to live their true essence. I knew my story was transformational, but I didn't quite know what an impact it would have until I started receiving feedback. People were sharing their own stories of struggles and pain; I find it incredible knowing that there are compassionate ears out there. This is how we can make a change in attitudes towards mental health, self-acceptance, and self-worth.

I'm also a reiki grand master and this has allowed me to deliver guidance and not just by telling my story. I am able to share my knowledge and empowerment to a wider audience. The true essence of my purpose is to help people break the stigmas and limitations that are preventing them from being their true selves.

Knowing we can live a life free from the chains of our past; liberate ourselves from thoughts and patterns that no longer serve us and speak from our true authentic self, is what motivates me to make a difference.

If I could speak to my younger self, the most important thing I would say is this: Be kind to yourself, always. Society's pressures are not yours to carry. Know you are beautiful as you are.

You are able to reach me by email; tulsi@hotmail.com and my website www.tulsivagjiani.com . My Instagram handle is @tulsidivine108.

# Tulsi's Conversation

When I was 10 years old, I was in a plane crash.

I sustained 45% 2$^{nd}$ and 3$^{rd}$ degree burns to my face and body. I awoke in a hospital in the UK with no recollection of what happened to me. I was clueless about the severity of my burns.

At first, after the accident, I felt exactly like the same person I was before my accident. I was still the feisty, confident, carefree young girl with ambition and a passion for justice.

However, I quickly learnt that my whole life had turned and flipped 180 degrees. Everything had changed.

Before my accident, I'd lived life like any other 10 year old. I never had to question my appearance or body. I looked like all the other 10 year old girls I knew. I had never experienced bullying relating my size, height, or looks.

Since my accident, it has been quite the journey. But I have grown through my experiences and have learnt the true meaning of body confidence.

I now know for sure that body confidence is something that we are all fully entitled to and deserve. Body confidence is an important part of self-respect and self-care, and there is no such thing as an unworthy body.

I want to walk you through how I have developed love, respect and gratitude for my body—regardless of the challenges I may have had along the way—and I want to help you do the same.

For as long as you are alive on this planet, your body is the only place your soul has to live. Therefore, it must be treated with the respect it deserves. I want to reassure you that your body is perfect just the way it is, and, although you may want to change things along the way, you can feel confident and worthy in your own skin regardless of where you are.

So let's pick it up again with 10-year-old me.

"Tulsi," a nurse said, "we are going to remove the bandages from your eyes." She was in charge of the burn unit at the hospital.

"It may feel slightly strange at first," she continued, "but take your time opening your eyes."

Why would it seem strange? What does that mean? I wondered.

I was confused. I felt scared. They kept telling me about these burns. I wanted to see them for myself. How bad could it be?

I felt the same on the inside. For me, nothing had changed at all.

I asked to see myself right away.

"Are you sure you want to look in the mirror?" questioned my nurse.

I was sure.

The nurse held up the mirror and I remember feeling quite excited to see myself, although the more everyone questioned whether I was ready to do this, the more apprehension grew in the pit of my stomach.

I looked in the mirror and I stared in shock.

Who is that person in the mirror? Certainly not me!

Did someone draw on my face as a joke?

It had to be a joke!

As I blinked and moved my mouth, so did the person staring back at me. It was at that point I realised what the mirror was telling me: the truth that had become my new reality.

That person in the mirror was me.

I was shocked and scared.

Little 10-year-old me did not recognise the person staring back at me. My face and body were severely burnt and bared no resemblance to myself.

My mind rushing, I instantly searched for a solution. "I know with some surgery and magic cream the scars will go away and I won't look like this forever. I can deal with this, it's only short term and soon they will vanish."

Time in hospital felt safe and I never had to question my looks or the impact that this would have on me.

But when I left the hospital to resume my normal life, the bullying began.

During my journeys to and from hospital and school the name calling began. People would cross the road in case they caught whatever I had, and there was constant staring.

It was difficult to comprehend what it was about my scars that made people uncomfortable.

It was in these moments my low self-esteem started to form.

My relationship with body confidence became negative as I started to absorb the comments from others.

'Who is going to marry you looking like this?'

'You're getting fatter. No one will be your friend. No man will accept you.'

'No one will employ you looking like this. You can get a job as a street cleaner.'

These dialogues were on repeat, for every positive comment I got I processed it as 20 negative comments. I hated my body and was always covering it up with baggy and black clothes. I felt like an attraction when I went to community events, a great opportunity for more people to make remarks or ignore me.

I felt awful and worthless.

## Self-worth Leading to Body Confidence

We currently live in a world where there is vast pressure to look and be a certain way. From how much we weigh to how we dress, what our body type is, or whether our skin is flawless enough.

Social media has made this harder. It inspires people to compare themselves with what they perceive to be perfection. It makes it hard for us to see the beauty we currently have as we are constantly comparing and competing with other people.

Growing up, I felt myself wanting to look like the beautiful women in the magazines, but how could I if I was fat, ugly or even short? I just could not shake it.

I built myself to the point where I loathed myself and had no self-worth. I was so consumed with my scars that I was convinced I didn't deserve anything good in life. What was the point in going forward when nothing good would ever happen for me?

I smiled a lot, which was a false indication of how I was truly feeling.

At parties or events, I was the life and soul of the party, I showed off my huge personaility. People wanted to hang out with me. I wore a lot of makeup, concealing and covering up my scars.

For a few hours, I could be someone else! I would get home and I would feel empty and self-loathing again. I was not the tall girl in the club or the pretty woman at the bar and I certainly was not the girl who got any attention from the guys.

## No more hiding away

In 2014, I was at a camouflage makeup workshop and during the break the practitioner asked me if I wanted my colour matched. I accepted the offer.

I had played around with make-up, so I was excited to get this done.

We applied the make-up on my left arm, heavily burned, and I suddenly started to feel quite uncomfortable.

I could feel that I was going to have a panic attack.

The practitioner got worried. She actually thought I was suffering from a reaction to the make-up!

I told her it wasn't the makeup. It was the fact that I couldn't see my scars on my left arm.

The colours. The textures. The patterns. They were gone.

This was not my arm!

I said I needed it removed as I wasn't comfortable. As I wiped away the make-up, my heart rate started returning to normal. I could finally see my arm again.

This is the moment when I realised that I no longer wanted to cover up my face or body. I was no longer ashamed and had accepted myself and how I looked.

Nowadays, when I put makeup on my face, I don't cover my scars, instead I use it to highlight or enhance my features.

This is a huge weight off my shoulders. I am no longer trying to conform to society's norms or pressures. Instead, I embrace my differences and what makes me unique.

I threw away a lot of make-up when I got home. It felt liberating but scary at the same time. How could I leave my house without the full coverage? If I wasn't concealing my scars or dark pigmentation, then was I leaving myself open to be judged?

But I knew I needed to do this as I no longer wanted these chains hanging over my head. I decided I no longer wanted to hide and I needed to do this. Not only for myself for the many women who scrutinise themselves daily to be a certain way or measure up to this false image of perfection.

A new sense of confidence was unlocked within me.

It was nothing like I had ever experienced, a new-found power.

Even as I felt a huge weight lifted, I also felt a sense of responsibility that I needed to do justice by my message of self-acceptance.

It is difficult to explain what confidence or self-acceptance feels like but all I can describe it as is the liberation to just be yourself. To fulfill your purpose and stand in your own truth. To remain grounded despite the ground shaking below you.

The mind is so powerful and can distort so much from the truth. I convinced myself that I was unworthy of love, opportunities, or feeling beautiful. It felt fake to receive even the simplest of compliments. It was excruciating, and I was gripped by low self-esteem. I was just existing with no purpose or dream.

I modelled for Katie Piper's Confidence—The Secret at the Ideal Home Show in 2015. I did not comprehend what I signed up for when

I accepted the invite.

I was starting to enjoy the confidence that I had but to model in front of a crowd was quite surreal. However, like most things, I dove right in!

We had four outfit changes, including swimwear. I bravely took a bikini, which is something I usually only ever wore for massages, as part of the swimwear range for the show.

The first catwalk went well, but I was so nervous as I had friends and family in the audience and this was the first time I had worn a bikini in front of them. To my disadvantage—which in fact turned out to be a blessing in disguise—I was shorter than the rest of the incredible models, so I was in the front!

Everyone could see me and my body. I was on full show, proudly sharing my scars and squidgy bits, things I usually wanted to hide and not expose to criticism.

From this experience, and going on to do nine shows, I found a new sense of freedom. I do not need to hide myself in the hope I won't get judged, because judgment will always happen. But now I know it is not my issue but theirs. I now choose to take bikinis on holidays or areas where there is a swimming pool. I do get people staring but I make it worth their while!

This also prompts conversation with women whom I meet on holiday by the pool or beach, approaching me to congratulate me on taking ownership over my body and not adhering to those who are uncomfortable around me.

So, whilst you are going about being yourself, there are many who are looking in admiration and not out of judgement.

You may have planted a seed of confidence and hope in them. I have had many people who have shared their stories of low body confidence, often after having a baby or from surgery or from weight gain or loss. It really breaks my heart that they cannot see their beauty and strength in overcoming something so huge.

I understand now how frustrated people around me felt when I couldn't see my own beauty and strength.

I encourage my friends around me to take ownership of their own body and mind. It is not an easy journey because it means having to break those chains of conditioned thinking or cultural restrictions, which can be holding them back unknowingly.

This is not about flaunting the body but simply accepting the body as a beautiful piece of art.

I want to empower people to break those patterns which often stem from childhood, family, and culture, so that they can make better choices for themselves and fundamentally gain confidence in all aspects of their lives.

Lack of body confidence hindered so many opportunities for me. I never felt good enough to get a job or try new things, such as sporting activities and so I let my fears hold me back.

My lack of self-worth and low self-esteem really debilitated me, and I went through a tough stage of depression. I never spoke to anyone about it. No one around me had a clue because I kept it hidden as I was so ashamed.

I felt a complete failure and I'd rather people called me names than to reveal that I was struggling with depression. I used to smile a lot, so no one questioned how I really was feeling.

My family presumed I had coped with the loss and scars well, so they never felt the need to ask.

The number of people that must go through the same feelings of isolation astounds me.

Mental health is a huge, complex and intricate subject. But, in the past, it certainly wasn't as discussed as it is today.

Back then, I didn't know who I could talk to, be that person a professional or someone close to me. How could I reveal how much I loathed myself and felt ugly every day? Who would believe me? Was I a freak for feeling this way?

It makes me sad to think the child-me was going through this emotional turmoil alone and scared. I often go back to those moments and embrace that child and tell her: It will be ok. You'll develop your confidence. Hang in there! Now I practise self-love every day to help me heal from those years of feeling worthless and ugly.

Growing up, I always knew that I was different from others. My thought process was unique in the way I felt about what I saw as injustices.

They didn't stem from my family or anyone I grew up but something I had inside. In school, I stood up to the bullies. I fought for things that I felt were right.

Without my parents around during my teens, there was no one to guide or understand those feelings, I dismissed it and withdrew into my shell.

Now as an adult, working on my goals and confidence, I have re-discovered my passion for justice.

I have the confidence to stand up for what I believe in and the people I want to help. I stand for empowerment and breaking down barriers.

Confidence has many layers, but I associated it with body image and could not get past this. However, breaking the limitations within made me realise it is much deeper. With each layer peeling away, I further found my voice and courage, which has led me to live and work in my purpose.

In April of 2006, I was diagnosed with end-stage renal failure, I thought I was dying!

Everything that I was working on and had been through was all going to end.

Surely this was not how I was going to go, unfinished, unfulfilled, incomplete!

What I didn't hear from my consultant was that I had options. I wasn't going to die but my life was going to change yet again!

This was during my university studies, and for the first time I'd felt some self-worth. I felt I could do this, that I was good enough to learn.

For the first four months of being diagnosed, I was left feeling anxious and very tired. I was so hard on myself, all the while not accepting that it was my disease that was making me feel this way. I convinced myself I was lazy but pushed through the fatigue to get to university.

In August 2006, I started dialysis, which was a huge life changing experience. I was surviving by being plugged to a machine every night for eight hours.

My body was changing yet again, I had a catheter fitted into my abdomen, unsightly and ghastly, back to feeling ugly and hideous again. I wore clothes 3 times my actual dress size because I didn't want anyone to see it.

My skin began to change colour. I had lost weight, which wasn't exactly a bad thing, but I had no taste buds and I ate about as much in a day as a small child.

I was exhausted with the excess fluid I was carrying, as well as the toxins I had inside me. I was grateful to be alive, just. But this loneliness and uncertainty started creeping up on me again.

Being on dialysis meant I had to be very organised, so I used to set my laptop and textbooks on my bed and then set and connect onto my dialysis machine. That way I could complete my degree.

It was challenging especially as I was exhausted, battling my insecurities and going through this alone. It was the toughest as there was no one to help me set up my machine and the guilt of asking grandfather to help stopped me from asking for anything.

This was my problem, so it was easier if I just got on with it. That was my attitude from when I left the hospital as a child. I did not want to be a burden to anyone and the guilt was too intense to admit defeat.

Despite all of this going on for three years, I managed to pass my degree with a 2:1 grade. Short of first place by 1%!

I am good enough.

I am clever.

And I can do anything I put my mind to.

I found some confidence. Despite the hurdles, I knew I could complete something as big as a degree. My mind stopped me from achieving so much more.

In January 2009, I received a call from my hospital to say they had a kidney for me.

I was in shock and not prepared so was not sure what decision to make. I had a few minutes to decide, and, considering my blood group is rare, I said YES!

The transplant was successful.

I was so ill after my transplant, but I put it down to the pains of surgery and recovery.

Later I discovered my body was reacting to the immune-suppressant medication. I had an operation within two weeks of my transplant because the kidney had a cyst and was leaking urine into my body.

I felt so ugly, unlovable and very angry.

My life had been great on dialysis. It wasn't the best but I made it work. Now, how could I be so ill and in pain?

I could not feel my right leg post-surgery. It was completely numb. In fact, I couldn't move it at all.

I was so scared that I said to my surgeon that I was not leaving this hospital until I could walk unaided.

I was so anxious for many reasons. Firstly, who would take care of me if I couldn't walk? The guilt was keeping me awake at night.

Too exhausted to focus on my physiotherapy and walking, I wanted to give up. I wanted it all to end.

This moment I recall with so much pain, helplessness and defeated.

I'd never felt it like this.

I went through lonely nights, feeling defeated and in pain.

How will I get through this? This was too much to bear and I couldn't burden my family with this.

Despite all this, I managed to walk three weeks after my surgery, unaided!

On one of those nights, me sleepless with worry and guilt, it came to me:

**What I cannot control I must let it go to the universe.**

I was exhausted from carrying so much. I was so ill and constantly in and out of hospital.

I am not a bad person, I would reason, and have been following the care given by my consultant. The doctors were just as baffled as I was, because it was not something they had experienced before. I was that 1 in 100,000 they address in the medicine leaflet!

Once the medication settled and I started to build my strength, I felt better within my mind.

My spiritual practise started to take shape and I felt I was reaching for it to make sense of my life and the direction I was going in. I have used various therapies/treatments to help me be where I am today, grounded and vibrating on the self-love energy.

These are some of the therapies I have used to help me:

- Reiki
- 5-elements acupuncture
- Meditation
- Crystals
- Buddhist affirmations
- Modern spirituality
- Hindu Vedic books
- Mindfulness meditation

## The Destination: Acceptance

I further found confidence with my scars and body after meeting other fellow burn survivors and knowing I was not alone. I was able to see the beauty within these fellow survivors, which gave me the courage to accept my own scars and own my story.

I started to share my story to my fellow burn-survivor friends and then to various organisations. The more I shared it, I got so much support and encouragement to share it further. Every time I shared my story, the chains of shame, disgust, ugliness, and unworthiness weakened. Finally, I could value myself and look back with pride rather than sadness.

In 2013, I started my journey of self-love because I was lost and needed direction. This led me to accept myself, my story and my scars. It is in no way an easy journey or a quick fix, but—slowly—I was able to see my scars differently.

I noticed the patterns, texture and colour formations and slowly started to love them. Soon I started to make them feel a part of me.

I have accepted the whole me: Body, Mind and Soul. Each scar and trauma has led me to this point in my journey, where I can inspire and empower others to see their own unique beauty. This is not only reflected from the outside but comes from working thoroughly from the inside.

The self-love journey has certainly been a challenge. There are moments when it's exciting, often dark and lonely, quite scary, stepping over the fears, highs of excitement and lows of facing the truth. However, I would do it all again to be where I am now, vibrating on the gratitude of my life and experiences because I feel honoured to be walking this path of self-acceptance, enlightenment and empowerment.

I now share my story on a global scale to help and empower people to break these chains and to take ownership of themselves because they are enough as they are. We are not for everyone, but we are enough for ourselves.

We all have a story of struggle filled with highs and lows, but in sharing them we can not only empower others but also free ourselves from the chains of our past.

My body has gone through mainly ordeals, but now I look at it with complete awe and gratitude.

My resilience, willpower, and determination have helped me overcome many hurdles, but my body has nurtured my growth and education. I learnt to love my crooked smile, something I hid for so long. It was a huge barrier to me loving my smile. A good friend said that was one of my most endearing features on my face.

That which is our hang-up may also be the very thing that makes us beautiful to other people. Now I smile, crooked or otherwise!

Learn to love and appreciate your body. It is made up of unique attributes which makes you different to anyone else.

Why blend in when you were born to stand out?

# CHAPTER 2

# MOVING BEYOND FEAR

## By Nikolai

I'm based in Oslo and I'm passionately interested in personal development. After taking a degree and working as a bureaucrat for years, I ended up working in sales. Going into sales might have been accidental, but it turned out to be a great learning experience. Sales is the perfect arena for self-development, as I got to face my fears on a daily basis. Sales gives us the opportunity to become aware of and overcome our weaknesses in a very practical way. Now I'm working to recruit young people and teach them how to make their careers in sales. I am also teaching them how to break free of their limiting beliefs.

Personally, I'm just a regular guy who has had mental health issues. I know that there are many like me who struggle, and I think it is important to be open about this topic with those who experience the same difficulties, and I hope to do that on a regular basis in the future.

The best advice I've ever been given is to make a hobby out of being alone. By following this advice I learned a lot about who I really am. Answering this question without being able to say a job title, degree or my relationship status was very challenging for me. It was, however, very rewarding, as it forced me outside of the regular conceptions of the question "who I am."

I would love to connect and hear about who you are. Feel free to drop me an email at julsteensen@gmail.com.

# Nikolai's Conversation

We have all experienced fear one time or another in our life.

Fear is a natural emotion. Fear helps us make good choices in dangerous situations. Fear keeps us from going too close to the edge of a mountain ridge. Fear can, however, drive poor decisions in other parts of our lives. I am one of those people whose fear got the better of me. I have let it stop me from feeling good about myself, and I've let it lead me into depression and low self-esteem. I want to share with you how I have learnt to deal with fear in my life, what I have found to work well for me in the hope that it could work well for you too.

I believe fear plays a big part in how we view mental barriers. When fear drives us, it limits our perspective, and ultimately prevents many of us from achieving our goals. For example, have you ever found yourself procrastinating instead of doing things that you know are good for you? Do you ever feel restless, unmotivated, sad or depressed? Are you ever scared to make changes to your life?

I've experienced all of the above. From the outside my life looked complete. I had the degree, the job, the apartment, and a great girlfriend. However, I was lost. I was living in a state of fear. A fear of failure or the unknown. A fear of being judged by others, but most of all myself. And a fear of taking action. I was depressed, overweight and had other physical issues.

Thankfully, there came a day, well several days, where I got honest with myself and that gave me the opportunity to break my patterns, and deal with fear in a constructive way. By allowing myself to feel the pain behind the fear it led me to realize that I needed to change some things, but also that I was making too big of a deal of everything. I was really hard on myself.

I am just a normal guy who turned my life around, with applying simple tools to my life. As in my case, the fact is that many of us are not taught how to deal with depression or other mental struggles before we find ourselves in them. Avenues like therapy are of course helpful and incredibly important- you should always seek help. However there are things that you can do yourself to help you make changes to your mental wellbeing, and it doesn't have to cost you anything either. I know that there are many like me who want to achieve a free-flowing life, while reaching their goals at the same time. If you are one of them, keep reading.

There are certain tools that have helped me immensely, I will share them with you over the next few pages. You can practice them individually, or put them together into a morning routine to start your day. The results of putting it together in a morning routine has been invaluable for me. You might cringe at the thought of getting up early! I hear you! I felt the same way, but after trying and experiencing myself, it completely changed my day and I found myself doing it willingly after a short time. In the beginning, before the habit is there, it might be some resistance, and that is okay. Let it be, and watch how it transforms your day as well.

## The Go-To's

The three go-to tools that have changed my life and mental well being are:

1. Meditation.
2. Visualization.
3. Exercise/Yoga.

## Meditation

Meditation is the most important tool I have. Through meditation I got to see how my fears had been making decisions for me, and by doing so, I was able to manage my fear. Not only that, meditation gave me a chance to see what was really going on. What was going on inside of me. Meditating helped me out of depression and also had ripple effects into all areas of my life, like my health and career. Meditation is so easy, and best of, it's free.

I believe this tool is so effective that everyone who applies it will benefit greatly from it. But, don't take my word for it. Try it out for yourself. Meditation is universal and anyone who experiments and develops skills in it will learn to sow good seeds, and take away the bad ones as well. In addition, meditation trains your concentration, keeps you calm in stressful situations, and creates awareness on how the mind works, and how it affects the body.

Previously I was always skeptical about things like meditation. I had certain preconceptions about it, I really let myself down by having these beliefs though. By accepting and allowing myself to be open to what so many individuals have benefitted from before me, I was able to benefit from it myself. It's okay to be skeptical, but being aware of why one is skeptical is key. If you are skeptical, please ask yourself why this is. You might be surprised by the answer.

Awareness is key, and so is knowledge. There is ample scientific research available at your fingertips these days that will help calm the analytical mind. If you are anything like me, I encourage you to do your own research so that you have more belief in the benefits of meditation before you actually experience it yourself. But in the end, meditation really just needs to be practiced.

## Practice

There are a million ways you can practice meditation, and there are no right or wrong ways. However, the breath is always the key component. Personally, I've found two methods to suit my needs.

The first one is available at anytime, anywhere. You just follow the breath. Focus on following the breath moving from the tip of your nose, feeling it in the back of your throat as it goes down, and at the end feeling the stomach expand. Then follow it back up again. Repeat. The idea is to quiet the mind by focusing on the breath. The mind will still come up with thoughts, this is to be expected. It might prompt an emotional response, this is good though. This is an opportunity to let go of some unwanted seeds. When you catch yourself thinking about something, and feeling a sensation, stay with that sensation until it goes away. Then just go back to the breath, non-judgmentally. This was hard for me in the beginning. I got upset and judged myself for not being good at meditating, all the while missing the opportunity to observe the feeling in my body.

Why do I mention being non-judgmental? Being in a state of non-judgement towards yourself simply feels good. This is neurochemistry in motion, and you let the emotions run its course in the body, and then you go back to the breath. By staying in a state of non-judgement you get to observe which thoughts you find yourself in, how you got there, and how you react while being detached at the same time. Then simply go back to the breath.

You can sit in a regular chair, or you can sit crossed legged with a straight back. I use both. The benefit of sitting in a crossed legged position with a straight back, is first of all that you won't fall asleep. The second one is that you will experience some sensations in the body by sitting in that position for a period of time. These sensations can be viewed as pain, or, they can be viewed as an opportunity to let go of your attachment to those sensations. By focusing on those sensations, non-judgmentally, you will see that you view pain simply as a sensation after a while. You will not let it affect you, and the sensation magically disappears, meanwhile you go back to the breath.

It is important to mention that there is no forcing here. If the sensation becomes too much and you feel the need to move into a different position, or just to relieve an itch, simply become aware of the sensation, take a breath before you take appropriate action. By taking a breath before, we train ourselves to act instead of react. This will automatically translate into your life when you meet a challenging situation. For example when our spouse does something that is annoying to you, or, you face a difficult situation at work, you have trained yourself to become aware and take appropriate action. You bring the state of awareness from you meditation into your daily life.

## Visualization and creating beliefs

Meditation calms you down, and gets you to the place where you have clarity. We want to use this clarity to create our desired change. It is normal to meet resistance in ourselves when we set out to create change though, and we might encounter thoughts like "what if I can't do it". It's like going to the gym for the first time in a long while. The fear of failure, or the fear of the unknown elicits an emotional response that can keep us from actually doing what we want.

Having fear is not a sign that we should not do it. It's often the other way around. What is worth doing is often outside of our comfort-zone, and when we try something new it's normal to fail. It's like a child who is learning to walk. The child does not master it at once, and the parent does not stop encouraging just because their kids falls down. Thus, failing is not dangerous. Failing is just a lesson for us to grow. By viewing failing in this way we make ourselves equipped to deal with problems that inevitably will arise.

Going outside of our comfort-zone can be uncomfortable. The main purpose of the brain is to protect us, to keep us alive with the fight or flight response. This is our ego talking and trying to stop us from changing because - well, we're alive. Don't screw that up. As the saying goes 'if it ain't broke don't try to fix it!' Alive is fine, don't get me wrong, I'm very happy to be alive, but being alive is not always living.

To overcome the fear of failure, or the fear of the unknown, we can create a belief in ourselves and in our desired outcome. It's like planting a seed and letting that seed grow in our minds. It doesn't matter where you are now, we all have this capability. To show you how easy and effective this is, let's do a short exercise together.

Close your eyes and imagine the following:

Open your refrigerator and pick up a lemon. Now put it on your cutting board on your kitchen counter. With a kitchen knife you, cut a big slice of lemon. Take that slice of lemon in your hand and look at it. Look at the skin and the fleshy part of the lemon. With the image of that slice, open your mouth and take a bite. When you bite down let the juices of the lemon flow and swirl around in your mouth with the help of your tongue.

What happened? Did you get any sensations in your mouth? Did you experience the bitterness and/or did you produce more saliva?

Now imagine the effect of doing this day after day, only with your goal you just created in mind.

We see people who are performing at high levels using this inherent human quality all the time. Coming from Norway, I was always fascinated by the alpinist on the top of the slope rehearsing in their minds the slope they were about to embark on. Why do they do this? It must have some positive effect on their results, otherwise, why bother? So, if it works for athletes to get results, why can't we apply this in our own lives? What they're doing is preparing their mind for what comes next. It's brain-talk and they are telling their mind that this is how we are going to do it, and it is going to be okay. "Look, we can do this!". "We just did it!". It lets us move beyond our fears. The mind does not know the difference between what is real and what is not real, if you manipulate it enough!

By visualizing what it is that you want, you'll create belief in both yourself and in your goal. Your mind will automatically look for opportunities to make that vision a reality, and act upon that. I would recommend making it a part of a morning routine where you visualize for 10 minutes, but you can do it at anytime and anywhere.

## Yoga / Exercise

We are living in an age where we can do, have, or be anything that we want. We have all the information we'd like at any time. It's at our fingertips. We're on the phone from the moment we wake up. When we take the bus we're on the phone. When we're with people we're on the phone. Don't get me wrong, our phones are fantastic, but it can be overwhelming, and this flood of information can prevent us from focusing on what we want.

As we already covered, the brain tries to hold us where we're at are because we're alive. Aside from the fact that this might hold us back, we also have an overflow of information, and our focus can get bewildered because of this. If our focus is scattered throughout the day, it becomes a habit to stay there. If we're scattered it's hard to take any action, let alone the right one.

The fear of taking action often comes from past experience, but more importantly, I think it comes from a lack of clarity. With the clarity from mapping down what you want and visualizing it, it becomes easier. We still want to add some energy and focus into that mix though.

We all know that exercise is good for us. It releases endorphins and gives us more energy throughout the day. So, exercise is great in any case, but if I could choose one exercise for the rest of my life, it would be yoga. Not only is it a great stretch, strengthening and cardio exercise, it trains our focus.

In my yoga sequence I have to focus. Holding a posture for an amount of time is no joke some days! It can even be boring. My mind will scatter and start thinking about something else, and I will lose the posture.

Yoga helps overcome the sensation we get when we're bored.

When we're bored, we tend to do other stuff, to alleviate us from the boredom. Yoga trains us to stay in a posture despite it being boring sometimes, thus strengthening our ability to focus on the here and now. Just as meditation, yoga helps us connect to our breath. We can take this with us into our busy lives, and our breath then becomes an anchor to overcome boredom and for us to stay present and focused on a task that we know must be done. We automatically become more focused through the practice of yoga. It's also a great exercise, and it's free.

You can do yoga no matter what level you're at. There are all types of free instructional videos on the web, too.

## Tracking your results

I encourage you to track your improvements because the brain can misremember. Simply reflect and write down your improvements. This is great for a confidence boost. You could, for example, write about how you reacted really well to a challenging situation where you usually would have reacted badly. Maybe you smiled or laughed a lot more or had more energy and found it easier to do things. Perhaps you did something that scared you, and that felt great afterwards. Or, under a meditation you realized a pattern, fear or belief that you hold, and you now know that this is something you can work on. Maybe you could hold your focus and concentration for a lot longer than before, and you see that what you have envisioned is starting to take shape.

By tracking your accomplishments you will come to see that the changes after practicing the three go-to's are not coincidental. When your mind tries to say that enough is enough of this mumbo-jumbo you will have enough leverage to keep going. You might even get more out of your practice.

This has been hugely effective for me. I have done what only a few years back was completely inconceivable to me. Things where fear would have gotten the better of me, and I would have stayed in my comfort-zone.

For example, I've always been slow in the mornings. After I started meditating for 20 minutes in the morning and evening, I was up at 5 a.m running in the park. This was after just one and a half weeks of this routine. I couldn't believe it. In addition, I was calm, and was way more effective during the day.

I was overweight. At most I weighed 97 kilos. Now I weigh between 70-75. The last 15 kilos I dropped happened after I started meditating, and it was enjoyable! It happened quickly and without all the struggles. The known struggles with lifestyle changes are in our minds, and by meditating one clears away the fog. I've tried a lot of different things up till this point to lose weight and to stay healthy, but the fog was always there. It was a struggle. There was a lot of fear involved in this process for me. I believed that it was too difficult and that I couldn't do it.

I picked up yoga and learned to stand on my head. For an old and stiff footballer this was impossible for me to even imagine only a few years back. The fear of standing on my head was a good one to overcome. To this day, I stand on my head to remind myself of how I I overcame fear.

I once got challenged to eat a Habanero (a strong chili). Not knowing how to deal with the pain or sensation I sat down and meditated. And, while people were probably staring at me like "who is this crazy person," I discovered that the burning sensation of chili is just an illusion. When I surrendered and allowed the sensation, the sensation passed. Without mediation I would have been running around screaming like everyone else!

Meditation made me realize that I wanted to change careers. I quit my job as a bureaucrat and started as a door to door salesman and earned more money than before.

The three go-to's have changed my life from a place of depression and despair to a place where I know that I can deal with my life. It has changed countless other lives.

That is the message I hope you have received from reading this. The three go-to's have taught me so many things about myself that I was not aware of. It really dialed in how our emotions and fears can drive our decisions. By changing these with simple and free methods we can go into unchartered waters with a sense of calmness.

Now, doing a headstand or eating a habanero might not be for you. That is fine. Only you can decide what you want to do. What I can tell you is that meditation, visualizing and yoga have the benefit of allowing one to see things in a totally new perspective. By having new perspectives you open up to new opportunities and you deal with challenging situations in a more productive way. And if you find yourself in an uncomfortable place while taking action towards your goals, know that you are doing something right.

Just take a breath and let the emotion pass.

# CHAPTER 3

# THE STORM THAT CLEARS THE PATH

## By Ben

I am a life coach, business mentor, and founder of the personal development community Shape Your Destiny.

I help driven visionaries maximise their genius and I live to help dynamic leaders amplify the impact of their message to the world. My speciality is a powerful conversation that offers a potential shift in perspectives and alters life trajectory.

My passion is witnessing people overcome their own challenges to live a life of fulfilment and purpose through deep inner transformation. My belief is that everybody has a right and ability to create to live a high quality life and what really lights me up with joy is seeing that moment in a person's eyes when they realize their true potential.

If I could go back in time and speak to my younger self I would tell him with absolute certainty to believe that he can create anything he sets his mind to. I hope you enjoy my contribution to the book sharing some of my life experiences and welcome you to get in touch by email, which is <u>Ben@Benallsop.com</u>.

You can also connect with me on all social media platforms and via the Shape Your Destiny community.

# Ben's Conversation

If you picked up this book and are currently experiencing challenges, then this chapter is presented to you with the hope that my journey inspires you to keep going, and to help you choose to bring your best version of you to the world, whatever that looks like for you.

I have come to learn that in chaos, turmoil, and pain that we can find our greatest gifts to the world. Those greatest gifts come when we keep going, prepared to face the most challenging parts of our life, even when we want nothing more than to give up.

Throughout my journey, I have discovered that life doesn't always give you what you ask for, but it always gives you what you need for the greater good in that moment.

When I was initially asked to contribute to this thought-provoking book, my heart's immediate instinct guided me to talk to you about overcoming adversity to move into a powerful state of being and go on to create a life of stability, and perhaps even enjoying a new found lease on life.

In my relatively short time on this earth I amassed some unbelievable experiences, many of which I never thought I would ever experience, some of which at one time I wanted to forget but have now chosen to accept as my path. And for the last 4 years I have obsessed over the workings of the human mind and what makes human beings do what they do.

Because when I was suffering and in pain, a part of me came alive. Long periods of darkness will either make you or break you, I chose the former.

By 37, I had experienced some of the highest of highs and the lowest of lows.

To tell you more about me. I am the eldest of 3 brothers raised in Manchester, I had a stable upbringing, I was a straight-A student. I became English Champion at Karate.

At 17, I struggled massively with my mental health, even attempting suicide.

I became a father at 23. I was also dependent on drugs, alcohol and partying throughout my 20's and 30's. I created a thriving global business by the time I was 30. However, following a string of very painful relationships, and the excruciating separation from my son's mother and subsequently the breakdown of the relationship with him… I almost decided to end it for a second time.

I remember the exact moment when my life started to shift.

I was 33. My business was crumbling, I was living a party lifestyle, I had just met a woman that ticked all my "boxes." On the outside I had built an image of a very successful man. I was driving the latest sports cars, wearing expensive watches, and living a life of luxury. I was just a normal person trying to chase success.

Waking up one morning after months of rushing about trying to keep the business afloat, I was greeted by the terrifying news that one of our major customers had stolen goods worth £250,000 from me, which were in a warehouse in Italy. I couldn't breathe.

The shock, horror and fear at the idea of losing it all. Then the phone call came… The goods weren't insured.

F***, what am I going to do? That was my instant response.

As I walked downstairs to tell my girlfriend, the world was spinning. I worried that she would leave me, I knew I was nothing anymore without the money. I knew that this was the final straw.

As I walked into the kitchen she saw the pained and terrified look on my face.

"What's wrong?" she asked in a kind tone.

"It's all gone," I responded. "They've stolen everything, I've lost it all."

"What do you mean?" she looked at me with a confused face.

"It's all fucking gone. I don't know what to do." I slumped in the chair.

I stayed slumped in that chair for a majority of the next 18 months, festering in my own thoughts.

All of it was gone. Any hope I had of recovering the business shattered, and I was left very stressed about what to do. I had no idea how events were going to play out and I was consumed by worry and fear of what might happen.

My immediate thoughts were to hunt this guy down and get my money back. In the background, I couldn't help but wonder how I was going to recover from this situation. I felt so much pressure that I couldn't think straight. How could this be happening to me? Why did things like this always happen? Why me?

To my surprise she didn't leave me. Instead, gave me a priceless gift I will never forget. It was during this time in my life that, through her care and love for me, she introduced me to the world of personal development.

Little did I know, looking back today, that this would be a defining moment in my life. Little did I know that the principles that were about to be introduced to me would change the path of my life forever.

I remember being skeptical. I remember terming it as bulls**t. I remember sitting there and listening to it and listening to her share the idea of a complete stranger telling me how to live and how to be happy and I rejected the idea completely.

No one will tell me, I thought.

She convinced me to indulge her and her ideas. Like anything in life, when love is involved, we are prepared to do whatever it takes. I was.

So, as I sat there on the front row at my first personal development event, listening to the speaker present, I could just feel that there was something more to this, and I was compelled to listen further.

I listened intentionally. It sounded like he had experience in overcoming hard times, and I was in hard times. I wanted to learn how to change those times.

That was the beginning of a 4-year obsession of understanding my own mind, with the inner workings of me.

I wanted to know why this was happening to me, I wanted to know why I had to suffer. Why I had attempted suicide as a teenager and why everything seemed like it kept going wrong for me. I wanted to feel good. As I started to learn about myself, I also started to learn it wasn't just me that suffers. So many of us do, in different ways.

I consider myself to be someone who is very resilient. I remember a time when I nearly gave up, and I can say that I now consider myself very fortunate to have the opportunity to write this.

There have been many times in my life when I thought that my situation was hopeless, that nothing was working out for me. I found that there was a shift in thinking, a shift which allowed me to move past that moment with renewed energy and strength.

This was one such situation.

In amongst those insanely painful days were the roots of new beginnings taking shape.

I am a believer in miracles. One of my favourite quotes is a quote by Albert Einstein,

"You can live your life as though nothing is a miracle or you can live your life as though everything is a miracle." I used to dismiss any idea that life was working for us, I had experienced too many troubling and distressing times for there to be some bigger plan."

In this moment, it felt like everything was gone: my money, my cars, my love, and my son. The bailiffs were pursuing the rest of my houses. I was living back in my hometown, back where I started, having to struggle. This was rock bottom.

Literally for the 100th time in my life I stood in front of the mirror staring at myself. I couldn't even bring myself to look at my own face. The anger at the world and the self hatred seeped to the surface, and then that was it, I broke down. I sobbed uncontrollably, with tears running down my face. I could feel myself giving up, thoughts spinning around my head. This is it, I thought. I have had enough.

Instantaneously, my thoughts switched to my son. How could I even think about giving up? He needed me. As I stood and looked at my tear-drenched eyes, I remembered that this wasn't about me. My life was much bigger than just me. I had to stay for the others I loved.

Twenty years of hurt, in that moment, built up like a colossal wave, and there was a decision I needed to make.

Sink or swim. Give up or decide to **never ever give up ever again.**

I thought about all the times I had suffered. I didn't want to suffer anymore. I wanted to be free. It was in this moment that something inside me changed. By now had started working with life coaches, mentors and specialists in the field. I was managing my own personal development and heard so many talking about turning around adversity, then going on to a better life, that I started to redevelop my awareness and knew it was possible.

I started to remember how talented and capable I was. I had created results in my life before. Why not this time, I thought? Embracing what I learned from the events I had attended, immediately there was a shift in the way I saw the world.

Shortly after this, a late summer morning, the sun was just rising and I sat by the lake in the park practising my now-daily gratitude ritual. Marcel, my trusted French bulldog, sat beside me.

This particular morning, I was finding it harder than usual to shift my negative thoughts of loss and abandonment, and as I drew in a deep meditative breath through my nose I heard an elderly man's voice.

"Are you ok?" he said.

"I have had better days" I replied.

"Beautiful morning though, do you mind if I take a seat?" he asked, indicating the end of the bench.

"Of course," I said, wishing he didn't, and wanting him to leave me alone to wallow in the story of personal loss I was currently playing out.

The gentleman was around the same age as my dad, carrying a walking stick and sporting one of those old style flat caps.

"You know I have been coming here now for the last 16 years, and I have gotten to meet some people going through some situations," he started.

"Oh really? I have lived here all my life myself as well," I replied. He introduced himself as David, and as we started conversation, I started to open up about my story.

"So what's your story, David?" I asked.

"Well let's just say I have been where you are now."

"What do you mean?"

"Ben, it's not difficult to see. We have all had those staring out at space moments where you don't know where your life is taking you. I remember breaking up with my wife almost 23 years ago now. It was the second hardest thing I have ever had to deal with."

"What was the first?" I asked inquisitively.

He responded, "Well lets just say some things no one should have to experience. My son, who was 17 took his own life."

I sat there is disbelief. My mind immediately raced to my own experiences. I remembered how I had just wanted to end it all. I remembered how frightened and afraid I was that night. In that moment I was 17 again.

Dumbstruck, I sat there as he continued.

"Just the most painful thing you can imagine. I don't think he ever recovered from the breakup between his mother and I."

As I absorbed the full story, All I could think about was the unbelievable set of coincidences that had brought David to the chair where I was sitting at the exact time I was sitting there to share this story with me.

I think that when we look closely at our experiences of life, there is some evidence of a thread of connection that runs through every single moment in our lives. Something calling us, something that we are meant to learn and quite often when we ignore that thing, life has a habit of slowing us down to make sure we find the lesson.

As David spoke, I simply could not believe what I had heard. In that moment, complete strangers had a conversation that changed both of our lives. As I shared with him my full story and what had happened throughout the course of my life, I could see the look in his eyes change as he realised just how much the story of his son had resonated with and affected me.

Completely forgetting about my own pain whilst talking to him, I realised that this was no coincidence. This conversation was meant to happen. I no longer had a sense of pain for what I was experiencing, but now had a sense of purpose in the realization that people needed help. We are all hurting in our own way in our own moments and I could use what I had learnt to wake people up from their suffering.

The gratitude I felt in that moment.

"Thank you David, thank you for sharing this story with me. I know it might not mean much to you, but hearing the fact that you have been through these experiences and now sit here today and sharing such a life changing story with me gives me strength. It gives me faith in this path, and makes me realise that this is much greater than me. I want to thank you with all my heart for having the insight and courage to share your journey with me so vulnerably. This has changed my life."

As we stood there together, I could see him getting emotional. I reached out to embrace him, and we hugged.

I only ever saw David one more time.

I was walking through the woods on my usual route. I reached in my pocket to find my Ipod, which was loaded with mediations, audiobooks and motivational tracks that I had spent a good day organizing and it was no longer there.

I kicked myself as I walked around the park, thinking that it was lost. As I was walking home, David was there.

"Ben, have you lost something?" In David's hand was my Ipod.

Some things are unexplained in life, and I don't think they need any explaining. What I do know, is that all of us have defining moments in our lives.

It's in these moments that we get to choose our destiny, through what we see and what we choose to believe. That day, I chose to believe that life is always working for me, even in those difficult moments when it seems like it's not, it's is always working out for the greater good.

The greater good in this situation is that I made a decision that my purpose on this planet was much greater than I ever thought possible. I made a decision that day that I would do whatever it takes, whatever is humanly possible, to ensure that no one else had to suffer like I had.

And this is where it really started.

This is where I really remembered what my purpose in life was. If I chose to leave, who could I help? If I chose to give up, who would be inspired by me? If I choose to live an average life, how could I be a good example to my son? I had to make a choice to take total responsibility for my life. The highs, the lows, the moments. All of it.

In that process, going back through my life's experiences, as I looked at that through different eyes, I started to realise that my whole life had brought me to this moment.

Could it be possible that all of life's experiences are designed to help us discover our true path in life?

What if all the moments of our life were working in harmony to bring us to a point where we could decide on the rest of our life and what we were going to create?

Just think about how many times you have come to a point in your life where you felt that it was all too much. Remember the moment you made a decision to keep going. We are all going to experience pain of some sort, I don't think any of us get through life without experiencing this in some way.

What's important in these situations is what we do with the pain. How we process and then act on these situations is the key. How we deal with the uncertainty of life. How we respond is what matters most. Our internal philosophy is what dictates the way we think and act in these situations.

If you sat there thinking... It's easy for you to say. You are not feeling what I am right now ... then please understand, when I say I was ready to give up, I really meant it. I had been struggling for almost 20 years. The fear, the pain, the shame and the suffering was unbearable.

I am not saying this for sympathy. I am saying this because, if you are reading this, then I want you to know that there is hope.

Believe me when I say I have experienced the worst pain I ever thought imaginable and I am still here to tell the tale. I remember making a decision that It would not matter what happens in my life that I will always remember how blessed I am.

I wake up every day saying "I am blessed". I remember looking in the mirror making a decision to never, ever quit, no matter how bad it seemed. I committed myself to waking up and finding something positive in every day. And, if I couldn't find something, then I would create it. I remember learning to feel grateful for everything, every moment of love, passion and joy, and every moment that came along to make me stronger.

It was difficult, it is difficult, and it will be difficult for you too. But it will be worth it. Life is always working for you, think about it and really embrace what that means.

Think about times in your life when something has happened without explanation or reason but when you look back it has come along to give you a deeper understanding of the path ahead. We all have these moments but it's what we do when we look closer at them that matters.

It is my hope that this chapter reaches you to let you know that you are not alone. That in reading my story you realize that no matter what you are going it through it's ok.

It doesn't matter how dark it seems.

Brighter days are coming. For those of you who have been taught to struggle and suffer in silence, life doesn't have to be this way.

I want to remind you that it's ok to ask for help. It's ok to have a conversation about what you are afraid of, and it's ok to talk about the challenges you might be experiencing.

There is so much support available to you if you start seeing things differently. So many of us, especially men, have been raised with the idea that opening up about our challenges is weakness. But exactly the opposite is true.

It is my hope that in reading this you find the certainty you need to know that whatever you are going through is only temporary, because it is. Believe that one day you will look back on this time as the making of you, an opportunity to define your life and the true meaning of your experiences. It is my hope, that whatever you find the meaning that brings true richness and peace into your life.

# CHAPTER 4

# BUILDING YOUR MENTAL HEALTH IN THE ORDINARY MOMENTS

## By Hannah

I am a mental health thinker, writer, film maker and communicator, working in mental health, storytelling, and media since my student film in 1997. I help people by helping them to be conscious of emotions like fear and shame which can drive mental health responses. My mental health community, #mentalhealthartists, helps people to practice the art of good mental health by embracing the everyday.

Our manifesto is "Good mental health is an art built on the habit of catching and appreciating very ordinary little moments. Let's make some ordinary moments together." In our online community, we share tips, tricks and ideas for how to live more creative and confident lives.

The thing I am most passionate about in mental health is building people's confidence - this is what I apply to my individual, group, and social media work with everyone I have contact with. Mental health is a terrible robber of confidence and life expectations. I hope that by practicing it as an art, we can start to believe in ourselves. If you want to join #mentalhealthartists it would be great to have you in our community. And I'd love to hear from you if you want to reach out:

www.mentalsnapp.com for more info

www.bitly.com/mentalhealthartists to join the #mentalhealthartists community

Hannah@mentalsnapp.com if you want to say hi.

Twitter @mentalsnapp

# Hannah's Conversation

When we talk about mental health in everyday conversation, we usually focus on the negative and not the positive. So we focus on mental illness than mental wellbeing. This seems illogical.

On deeper reflection, it seems that this is less a problem about the way we treat mental health and more something that is systemic to the way that medicine views health and illness in the West.

Western medicine is about prevention and remedying of ill. Unlike traditions established in, say, India or China, where wellbeing and balance are prized, Western medicine is about identifying and isolating where the body or mind are going wrong, and treating that deviation from the norm as distinct from the whole picture of the mind and body.

Different nations have different views about medicine. America, for example, focuses on prevention for the rich and simply treatment in extremis for the poor. The NHS, in contrast, tries to provide a broad swath of treatment. However, the concept of 'illness' rather than 'health' still underpins each model.

I come to mental health from a different angle. I come to it not from a health/illness approach. I approach it like a storyteller.

I've been in mental health for twenty years, telling my own story on film and helping others tell theirs. I've talked to people who use mental health services up and down the country, and I've been in hospital and lived alongside other service users for periods of time. I've done this five separate times in my life. I've spent that time telling and listening to stories.

I've been in the field of mental health and story ever since I made my first films on mental health, full of anger about the way that I had been treated by the system.

At 21, I had to leave my university course due to mental ill health. My two year period of being role-less and stigmatised in society in the interim left me with my mental health making a hard-hob-nailed-boot imprint on my identity.

Even after I started making films, telling my story, and helping others to do the same, I felt the deep shame of self-stigma. That doesn't help your mental health. What does help, and what moved me away from the suffocation of self-stigma and shame was the simple act of telling my story. Mental health can be a connector, if the stories are told without shame.

The central issue is in recognising the value of individual stories, celebrating stories and championing voices. I know this because, in my twenty years as a mental health film maker, I've seen people time and again feeling heard, validated and coming away feeling better about themselves through the process of telling their stories on film.

I have to admit that I did not have such a positive response to it when I was first introduced to the idea of telling stories about mental health.

Twenty years ago, I was offered a job at Mental Health Media, the leading production company at the time for films about mental health. However, in recognition of the fact that at the time people didn't speak on camera unless they knew that the person behind it was sympathetic and had personal understanding, the job had a caveat. They wanted me to describe myself as a 'service user filmmaker'.

"A mental health film maker?" I scoffed at them, my putative employer. I'd only made one film on mental health at the time. "The two have nothing to do with each other. You might as well call me a mental health sock washer."

A couple of days later, a very nice note and a pair of new socks came through the post. I took the job. I've never looked back. I've spent twenty years trying to figure out what film and mental health have in common.

Telling stories is a powerful therapeutic measure. I'm all for finding your own voice. This has led me to some interesting places in the health/illness debate.

In my work I help people tell stories, and I present on the value of stories. I realise that there is the problem of shame and self-stigma in mental health. I also recognise that there is a more compelling problem.

It comes back to that lack of prevention and isolation of illness that is at the heart of the Western model of medicine. People don't know what good mental health looks like, they only know that they are in pain when they are feeling bad. They don't know what to aim for in order to feel good.

I have a little caravan retreat in Whitstable, where I go to think. I was there on a working retreat, trying to condense all the learning and thinking that I've done over the course of my adult life, managing my mental health into one summary statement. The reason I was doing this wasn't to define mental health. However, that definition is what I ended up coming to, sitting in my caravan, with the call of spring and an Easter holiday around me.

Suddenly, there on the pad in front of me, written in orange pen in the middle of the outline of a phone screen, had arrived fully formed a sentence that I knew I could meditate on, a definition of mental health.

It was based on Philip Larkin's poem, Born Yesterday, he wishes for his goddaughter and that she might be ordinary:

If that is what a skilled, flexible, vigilant, enthralled

Catching of happiness is called.

I love the idea of the life craft that it conjures up. I've been presenting on that poem for years while running Mental Snapp, my video diary app for managing mental health. It inspired the definition I came to, and that one sentence simply flowed through me, through all the thinking I'd done, and I just wrote it down.

Here is the sentence.

"Good mental health is an art built on the habit of catching and appreciating very ordinary little moments."

I write this as someone who has been in extremis with my mental health.

I've shot up into space in a massive hallucination, I've fallen out with friends and family and patched up again in dramatic scenes, and I've dealt with anger and addictive behaviour patterns. I've also consciously worked on my life craft skills.

Mental health is an art, not a science, as it is consciously experienced, and art has to be based on a discipline. Just as a single unit of a painting is a brushstroke, and of music the note on the bar, the single unit of good mental health is the experience of being in the moment, the ordinary moment. The discipline that stores up these moments to make them into something to base a life on, is to catch, consciously notice, and appreciate, or be grateful for, as many of them as can be.

I left my pad and went walking into Whitstable. As I walked I noticed butterflies on the cycle path that leads into town, the spring sunshine bringing out the buds of blossoms on the trees. I thought about the sentence, and I added to it in my head. The addition I had was from the group that I wanted to bring it to, I wanted to share it, and I wanted us to share ordinary moments. Community. That is what supports good mental health. The additional sentence I put on the end of that definition was all about that. "Let's make some ordinary moments together."

Six months on from that moment and we now have the beginnings of a community doing exactly that. We meet weekly to practice the art of good mental health. We throw a ball around, kick off the shackles of the week and check in with each other as to how we are doing that day. We sing together, we form a circle and around that circle we meditate on props and prompts that encourage creative thinking. We are making art, mental health art, in our circle. We are living with craft, living with that muscular arm that reaches up and plucks happiness from the tree, the one that Philip Larkin describes.

Come and join us. We've got an online community on an app, we meet every week, and we sing.

Each week, drumming on our hearts, we sit in a circle and we sing together 'This little light of mine, I'm going to let it shine'. Such a simple song, one that many of us knew as children. The very reverse of the shame that surrounds mental health. Drumming on our hearts keeps us powerfully in the moment - try it yourself when you're feeling skittish - and doing it in community even more so. It's all about those ordinary moments, consciously creating them. That's why the final sentence of the definition is a rallying call "Let's make some ordinary moments together".

In making ordinary moments together, we sit around in a circle, around a film reflector, which pops out as a circle and forms a natural stage for our conversation. We've taken individual words from that song, and meditated on them one by one. We've taken the word 'this' and meditated on it using props including some beautiful and uniquely formed fruit and vegetables, we've taken the word 'light' and done a meditation including candles and mirrors, we've taken the idea of 'little' and meditated using crepe paper hearts, big and small.

Anything can be a source of wonder, and it has led me to a different way of viewing the creative acts I'm making everyday just by the process of living. At the beginning of the workshop, we each take a name tag and write our name on it followed by the tag #artist. It's just to remind us that we are performing an act of creativity every day.

These are the ordinary moments with which we fill our lives.

There was a saying that I came across online recently. It ran "There are two ways to live. One is that nothing is a miracle. The other is that everything is."

The very first time we met as a group, we meditated on the phrase 'perfectly ordinary'. That idea came from a meditation and a piece of writing that I'd done, when I'd been walking along the road and saw a perfectly ordinary flower, a perfectly ordinary dandelion, a perfectly ordinary dustcart. There they were, how perfect, how ordinary, perfectly placed, just where they were.

For that first meditation in the group, I pulled out paper party decorations, that folded out into globes. Intricate paper, perfect in its ordinariness. We sat and breathed in silence together, made some notes, shared, laughed, sang.

Let's make some ordinary moments together. That way gratitude, appreciation, artfulness, community, connection and - most of all - good mental health, can truly lie. Enjoy connecting to the ordinary today.

# CHAPTER 5

# THE UPSIDE OF DEPRESSION

## By P.T.

I decided to write my story for this book because I hope by reading it it will give the reader strength to know that when you go to that dark place there is a way out, you just need to look for it. Selfishly I have also used this opportunity for it to become part of my therapy to accept what I went through.

If I could go back and speak to myself in 2015 it would be to say, 'Get help, you don't need to go through this alone. Speak to the people you trust. You are not alone and when you finally open up about it in the future you will realise that a lot more of everyone around you went through or are going through something similar'.

I really do hope that reading what I went though helps you if you're going through a tough time or feel yourself slipping into that dark place. I hope it helps you find a way out or stops you from going there altogether.

# P.T's Conversation

Experiencing depression was the best thing that ever happened to me.

When you have dug yourself into a deep hole, the light at the surface begins to disappear. Before you know it, it's gone.

You can't see a way out. You feel like you're suffocating in your own skin. At this point, one of two things happen: You either give up and break, or you fight and find a way to climb out.

I'm glad to say that I am one of those who managed to climb out. I can honestly say that I'm the happiest I have ever been.

This chapter is meant to inspire you.

If you are in the same position, if you feel like you it is the start of a downfall, if you are suffering with depression or poor mental wellbeing, as cheesy as it sounds, there is always light at the end of the tunnel. I found mine, as will you.

A few lines up, I mentioned 'digging yourself into that deep hole.' I understand, as many others should, that being depressed isn't a matter of choice.

For some people it's an underlying medical condition, past trauma, or another combination of factors that come together to make one feel that way. This is specific to my journey and it's how I feel I got into that place. I was responsible for all the decisions I made in life and they eventually led me into this feeling.

My mindset now has taken a shift to where I take responsibility for my actions and I understand that where I was and where I am now mentally is because of me. All the times I felt stuck and suffocated, I always had the power to change my circumstances and all it took was for me to take responsibility.

Again, this may not be the case for everyone. Many people strive to be positive but external circumstances or chemical imbalances can alter mental well-being.

I was 26, a professional working in the corporate world and newly married to my best friend. I had my own house, a nice car, a great social life, and a loving family. On paper, my life was damn perfect, as is the case for a lot of people with depression.

So what went wrong? Honestly, I can't be 100% sure. I know I wasn't happy with my job at the time and I dreaded going in to work every day. My life wasn't what I imagined it would be and I think this eventually became too much for me.

I know that people hating their job and feeling trapped in a cycle is a common sentiment, so why did it push me over the edge? Not many people live the life they imagined they would, so is everyone feeling the way I did deep down? I still don't have answers to these questions. But every day it was becoming a struggle for me until eventually it began to show.

Sometime in November 2015, I jumped awake in the morning. Before going to work, I woke up to a sensation of being unable to breathe.

My heart was pounding, I began to sweat, I felt like I had a huge weight on my chest which was trying to pin me down. It got worse, it felt like my heart was going to explode, I couldn't catch my breath no matter how hard I tried. I needed to get out. I jumped out of bed, ran into my bathroom and sat in the corner, hyperventilating. Finally, after what felt like forever, I started to calm down. I was confused. That was my first panic attack.

The second panic attack I had was in December 2015. I had the same experience as above but this time it did not stop. I had to call in sick to work.

From that point forward, it started to significantly affect every aspect of my life.

As the weeks and months went on, the panic attacks occurred more frequently. I got that same feeling of being pinned down to the bed with a heavy weight… a weight that only seemed to get heavier.

The relationship with my wife began to take a downturn. I stopped speaking to her about what I was going through and I withdrew from my friends. The only thing that seemed to bring me any happiness at this point was going back home to see my parents, even the comfort that was providing me was beginning to deteriorate.

My wife kept on telling me to go into therapy or to see a doctor before it got worse. All I kept thinking was how would that make a difference?

When you're in a withdrawing mindset, you don't even want to speak to those that are closest to you. Then to have to sit in a room with a complete stranger and talk about your deepest and darkest thoughts…that was not going to happen.

I think there may have been some male ego in there. I remember instances growing up and my dad telling me not to cry because that not what boys do, but I mostly put it down to just not wanting to talk to anyone, thinking what's the point and being a bit skeptical.

I can remember calling my manager at work one morning, crying down the phone, explaining that I wouldn't be coming in. I remember the worry in his voice as he asked me what was wrong and all I did was put down the phone. Very soon after this incident, I quit my job and started to work through an agency. I only accepted work on the mornings I felt able to go. This slowly dwindled down to one day a week.

I also had a rapidly declining social life.

As the anxiety got progressively worse, I found that alcohol made the anxiety symptoms dissipate. I started to feel anxious at random parts in the day, so coming home from work and having a couple of whiskeys in the evening helped ease the feeling.

The decline was fast. This soon turned into drinking in the morning, sometimes as early as 4am. Sometimes I had gone through a bottle of whisky before my wife had even woken up. She would come downstairs and I would already be hammered on the sofa. I can't imagine what it was like for her to see me this way.

I started to go into work extremely unkempt. I would shower but my hair wouldn't be in place and my clothes would be washed but wouldn't be ironed.

I always used to take pride in my appearance, but I just didn't have the motivation to do it. Just being alive was beginning to become difficult and I was losing interest in things that I used to love to do before. I lost my appetite.

And then thoughts of suicide started to creep in.

I started thinking I was a burden on my loved ones. They will be much better without me. What am I contributing to society and the world? Will anyone even notice if I'm gone?

These thoughts stemmed from a place of love and care. I loved those people even at that point in my life and I needed them more than ever but I convinced myself otherwise and that they were better off without me. What keeps you going in those moments and what kept me alive must have been a thread of willpower buried deep down and the hope that I supposed one day I could get better.

I remember sitting on the edge of my sofa after having a few drinks, a knife in my hand, just holding it there. In a way, the whole thought of it made me feel quite calm. It would only be a few minutes of pain and then peace forever. It sounded like a great deal. I didn't do it. I couldn't.

I'm so glad I came to my senses.

I suffered with these thoughts for around 11 months.

Then I had one incident which was my turning point.

In a drunken haze which I don't clearly remember, I had written a suicide note addressed to my younger brother. What I do remember is waking up at around midday after a long morning of drinking and reading something along the lines of, "I'm so sorry, please tell mum and dad that I wasn't a bad person and ask them to forgive me. Please look after my wife and help her move on. She deserves it." I couldn't read any more.

I broke down and cried so hard it felt like all the built-up frustration over the past 11 months was being released.

For some reason, reading that note hit me hard, and I had a tough talk with myself. I woke up from this haze I had been in and realised that I'm no good to anyone in this state. I felt miserable all the time. What was being like that going to achieve?

My parents came so close to losing a son, my wife a husband, and my brother almost lost his older sibling. Sitting here now, I put myself in their shoes and imagine how it would feel to lose one of them.

I needed to fix up. I was worth everything to them. It was time to realise my self-worth too.

I threw away the whisky, decided to take a break from alcohol until I felt much better and start the job of rebuilding myself.

I took my wife out to dinner and spoke to her about what I had been going through and promised her that I would go to see a therapist and work on myself. Furthermore, I promised her I would try my best to never go back.

A few months before I was given a book by a friend out of the blue called The Miracle Morning, and in that part of my life the book spoke to me and became central to my rebuilding process. It was almost a sign. I was being asked to better myself without even expressing my struggles.

I picked up meditation, started going to the gym, began kickboxing, started therapy, started eating properly, practicing gratefulness and visualisation, and began to educate myself. I have carried on most of these habits, except for the kickboxing and therapy, to this day, which helps me keep the anxiety at bay most of the time.

During my therapy sessions we spoke about my life and began to unpack and find the root cause for my anxiety and depression. My therapist also gave me techniques to deal with the anxiety symptoms. I found that incidents from my childhood were sources to my anxiety issues that I have now. The theory is that facing dangers as a child must have programmed a fight or flight response into my subconscious, which triggered itself around the times I felt vulnerable or threatened.

I chose flight when I was young. This carried through into adulthood. Work had become something which I had associated with negativity, so flight was my first response.

My life has completely changed, and my mindset has become much more positive.

I'm in a happier place now, however that dark place has never left me. After being much more open and speaking to others that have been through a similar experience, they too have said similar things, that the demons never leave you.

But I'm much more well equipped to deal with it now. If I do visit the dark place, it will be for an evening, but the next day I will be fine. I also don't punish myself for feeling that way anymore. I've just accepted it's part of me and have confidence that it will pass. I find it's much better to cope that way. If I feel overwhelmed during the day, I will try and take some time out to meditate or go for a gym session. That belief that it will pass gets me through these times.

I had never really taken the time to think about what constituted happiness for me. I knew what made me happy and what didn't.

But what did a happy life look like for me?

I had never asked myself the happiness question. I was just plodding along with my life and letting things unfold as they were. I have taken so much more time to reflect on what happiness means to me, and I think I have found the answer.

I focus much more on gratitude for all things small and big. It has given me a purpose to live for. Most of my days start at 5am now and I take the first hour or so for myself to read, do some meditating, etc. I feel much happier and it gears me up for the day. When my wife's alarm rings in the mornings I will go up to bed and kiss her good morning. Little moments like that bring me so much happiness.

It's important to say my wife also suffered during that 11-month period, too, and her mindset had also been affected. I'm ever so grateful she was in my life around that time and didn't leave my side. I can't thank her enough for all the support and love she showed me, staying awake with me when I couldn't sleep. She stuck by me through it all, which I will be forever grateful for.

I'm in a place in my life where I have been more driven than ever to achieve my goals, but I have also realised how important my family is to me. I have realised that my happiness lies in theirs. My goals come second to their happiness, having this perspective has also contributed to my own.

We're always told to go to the gym, eat right and look after our physical health. But we never get taught that our mental health is just as, if not even more, important as the physical side. You may have heard the following phrase before. 'If your physically injured, you see a doctor without question. So why don't we go to see a therapist when our mental health is "injured"?'

Why is it such a stigma? You should never struggle in silence and its ok to talk to someone if you need to.

I know of so many others that have been through the same situation but we never seem to talk about it. I can't recommend going to see a therapist enough. Although I haven't spoken about my therapy sessions at length, it was a huge part of my recovery and your journey to recovery will be specific to you.

The benefits of taking care of yourself, making your mental wellbeing a priority, and being grateful for the things you have—they should not be underestimated.

# CHAPTER 6

# IT'S OKAY NOT TO BE OKAY

## By Sophia

My name is Sophia and I'm a London-based Certified Wellness Coach for young professionals. Having suffered burnout whilst working in a corporate job, I'm passionate about helping others create a work / life balance. As a result, I also work with companies to implement Corporate Wellbeing programmes, particularly for the younger workforce.

One piece of advice I'd give my younger self when starting employment is to set your boundaries early on. Don't be afraid to take a lunch break, ask for holiday and leave the office on time. The earlier you set these boundaries the more comfortable you will feel at sticking to them. If you stay late every night in your first week with no work to do it is unfortunately likely to be expected of you going forward.

It took me a while to realise that the quality of your work is far more important than the hours you spend at your desk! But what if your company doesn't have this culture? Send them my way and hopefully we can fix it… If there is something in your life you'd like to change (or would just like to know more) I would love to connect with you. You can check out my website www.shinewithsophia.com, follow me on Instagram @shinewithsophia or email me at info@shinewithsophia.com.

# Sophia's Conversation

You are imperfect.

When I first heard these words, I felt my body tense up. I immediately tried to push the notion away. That inner, defensive voice screamed out, resisting this fact.

But, after a moment, I let it sink in. I felt an overwhelming sensation of comfort wash over me. I am, indeed, imperfect.

And so are you. As is everyone around us.

Brene Brown famously said in her TED talk on The Power of Vulnerability: "You are imperfect. You are wired for struggle. But you are worthy of love and belonging"

This quote really hit a nerve with me. For many years I believed that I had to be perfect in order to be worthy of love and belonging. If someone failed to call after a date, I would spend hours analysing every little detail. Had I overshared? Been too open? Said the wrong thing? I always concluded that they weren't interested because I hadn't been perfect.

But what did perfect mean? To me, it meant to always looking and feeling okay. Therefore, by default, I believed:

**Everyone = Perfect = Always Okay = Worthy of Love and Belonging**

A belief so entrenched that it still caused my initial resistance to any opposing ideology, as touched on above.

But, what I realise now, is that this couldn't be further from the truth. We are imperfect. We are wired for struggle. We are not always going to be okay. And this does not diminish us from being any less worthy of love and belonging.

My beliefs have changed:

**No one = Perfect = Always Okay = Worthy of Love and Belonging**

**Everyone = Imperfect = Sometimes Not Okay = Worthy of Love and Belonging**

It is completely okay to not be okay. In the words of Brene Brown once again: "Imperfections are not inadequacies, they are reminders we are all in this together"

But why do so many of us still feel ashamed to say we're not okay?

## We live in a society that craves perfection

According to the Oxford English Dictionary, perfection, in this context, is defined as:

- having all the required or desirable elements, qualities, or characteristics; as good as it is possible to be

- make (something) completely free from faults or defects; make as good as possible

But how do we know what the 'required' or 'desirable' elements are? How do we know what are 'faults' or 'defects'?

We naturally look for the answers in society.

As we know, the society we live in has become increasingly obsessed with perfection. Nearly all of the images we see in magazines and adverts have been photoshopped. And it doesn't stop there. Although the prevalence of photoshop on social media is not well documented, users now have the ability to edit their images on these platforms in some way through filters or selfie-enhancing apps.

Do the images we see ever tell the truth?

During an interview with the Washington Post, Zilla van der Born, the artist who faked a trip through Asia with photo-editing explained: "It is [so easy] to believe in a distorted reality. I wanted to make people more aware that the images we see are manipulated, and that it's not only the models in the magazines, but also our friends on social media who contribute to this fake reality... together we create some sort of ideal world online which reality can no longer meet."

No wonder we feel so pressured into hiding our truth and instead aim to perfect our images online and even our personalities in real life in order to 'fit in' with the rest of society. The irony is that everyone is faking it. Perfection and reality are not the same thing.

The idea that our lives have to be perfect through the lens extends even further to the rising trend of the health and wellness industry. Don't get me wrong, I believe this industry is having a positive impact on society in general, but there is a hidden underworld. What do I mean by this?

Let's take the example of my day below...

**<u>Tuesday, 3rd September 2019</u>**

05.00am: wake up and drink 2 cups of Tulsi herbal tea

05.20am: meditate for 20 minutes

05.40am: visualisation and positive affirmations

05.50am: write down 3 things I'm grateful for

06.00am: yoga stretch in the sitting room

07.00am: group fitness class - Barry's Bootcamp

08.30am: breakfast – acai bowl

09.00am – 12.00pm: send emails

12.30pm: lunch – quinoa and avocado salad with falafel and 1 cup of tulsi tea

13.00pm – 17.00pm: organise meetings and snack at 4, chocolate protein balls

17.00pm: read a book on my commute home

19.00pm: dinner – tofu and vegetable stir-fry and 1 cup of tulsi tea

22.00pm: bedtime

The day above is what I strive for. After reading the book, The Miracle Morning, by Hal Elrod, I was inspired to wake up an hour early and fit in meditation, affirmations, visualisation and yoga stretching, all before my day started. I feel great when I do!

However, in reality, sometimes I can't be bothered. I wake up tired, feeling lazy and I hit snooze until the very last minute. Or I'm too hung over to move.

What is annoying is that, because I strive to be healthy in all areas of my life, I now feel guilty when my day is not like the above. I look at the health and wellness professionals on social media who appear to be having every day like the one I've just outlined. So I get frustrated when I don't. But that isn't reality. Sometimes I just feel like rubbish and can't be bothered (despite being a Certified Wellness Coach).

For perspective, let's take Saturday 7 September 2019 as another example (after a particularly boozy Friday night dinner out with friends):

## <u>Saturday 7 September 2019</u>

07.30am: wake up - go back to sleep

12.00pm: wake up again and text friends in bed

13.30pm: move from my bed to the door to let the Deliveroo in (vegan Thai curry takeaway)

14.00pm - 22.00pm: lie on my sofa and binge watch the entire series of Euphoria whilst eating takeaway

23.00pm: bedtime

People are so quick to post and talk about the first example but less open with the second. But life is all about balance. So don't be hard on yourself!

I recently went to see Tony Robbins present in Dubai and he said that the most frustrating question he ever gets asked during interviews is, "Are you happy all the time?" His reply is, "Of course not!" But he has trained himself over the years to shorten the amount of time he spends in a negative state. Surely that is the goal.

So how can you shorten the negative and cruddy mindset?

**Firstly, talk with someone. Please just talk with someone.**

This morning, for example, I woke up and rang my best friend for a 5-minute cry. I don't know what I was so upset over, but I just needed to let it out and talk it through with someone. As soon as I shared how I was feeling, I felt fine again.

I'm not saying it is always that easy, but, for me, being open and vulnerable and telling someone how I'm feeling is the first step to feeling better.

It takes strength and bravery to allow yourself to be vulnerable and surrender to the emotions you're feeling whilst allowing them to pass through. Recognise that this state is only temporary. It also creates that open space for people to then share back with me when they are not feeling great. The more open we are and the more we share, the more we change the notion that we all have to fake being perfect in order to 'fit in' with society.

**Second, focus on something that brings you joy and fulfilment.**

This is different for everyone. For me, it is lighting a candle and reading a book. For others it might be painting, singing, playing or listening to music, cooking, dancing, running - something that you can completely absorb yourself in.

We are all born with a gift. When we use it and share it with the world, this is how we are truly fulfilled.

**Thirdly, give yourself the time to sit down in silence and meditate.**

I know it is easy to say, and not so easy to do. Meditation is truly a powerful and free tool which can be used by anyone to change your state and let the emotions pass through you in as short a time as possible.

It doesn't matter how much kale you eat or how much yoga you do, your outer world is always going to be a reflection of your inner world. If you do not allow yourself the space to stay present and grounded, it will always be impossible to find long-term happiness.

Doing meditation is like going to the gym for your brain. It quite literally stops the brain from producing so much cortisol, the stress hormone, and can have a huge impact on your current mood and thoughts.

I recently listened to Gelong Thubten on the Deliciously Ella podcast who spoke about the power of meditation. Gelong is a 21st Century Tibetan monk who recently published the book, A Monk's Guide to Happiness. Gelong believes happiness is a teachable skill, which can be taught through meditation:

"When we are searching for happiness, there is a sense of hunger, of incompleteness. We are wrapped up in the expectation of getting what we want, a fear of not getting it. Trapped in the uncertainty, we believe we can only be happy when our goals are completed, which means we are trapped in the future and not the present. Thoughts and emotions create a storm inside us. We are their slaves. Moment to moment we find ourselves in a fight with reality, constantly wishing things were different. Happiness involves mastering these thoughts and emotions and embracing things just as they are. It means we relax and stop trying to manipulate our circumstances. If we can learn how to rest deeply in the present, even when facing difficulties, we can train our mind not to judge but instead to discover within ourselves a tremendous force of happiness and satisfaction".

Another quote I love from Gelong is the following:

"Your own personal history of suffering becomes the thing enables you to help other people".

But it is all about consistently showing up and to live this amazing life in the best possible way you can. To recognise you're going to have rubbish days. But accept it when it happens. Because it is okay to not be okay.

Be curious.

Get outside.

Go to bed on time, some of the time.

Drink water.

Breathe from your diaphragm.

Eat broccoli.

Eat chocolate.

Get a routine baggy enough to live in.

Don't beat yourself up.

Be kind to other people.

And yourself.

Accept that not everyone will like you.

Appreciate those who do.

Remember the bad times don't last.

Don't be defined.

Allow mess-ups.

Want what you already have.

Look up to the sky.

Not just down to your phone.

Remember to be alive.

**- Matt Haig via his Instagram account**

# CHAPTER 7

# HOW TO LOVE YOURSELF UNCONDITIONALLY

## By Jamie

My name is Jamie and around mid 2018 the idea to create this book project came to me. All I wanted was to help someone else find the light at the end of the tunnel, the lemonade in the lemons, and to find hope where it felt there was none.

Outside of this book, my goal is the same, I want to help people find the best in themselves. I am a motivational speaker and speak all over the UK at events and I am the founder of Thrive by Thought.

Thrive by Thought is a resource hub, community and safe space for women to feel inspired, confident and empowered so that they can make the most of themselves and their lives.

I guide women to boost their self love and respect, change their perspective, quit self sabotage and embrace the absolute best version of themselves by working on their mindset. I help women to minimise self doubt and instead embrace fierce self love, self belief and true understanding of who they are and how much they are really capable of. Together we breakdown the boundaries in your mindset that are holding you back.

If I could go back, I would tell my younger self to quit the self doubt! I've really come to realise how we are each far more capable and worthy then we think we are and that it makes absolutely no sense to let our self doubt stop us from going after what we really want in life.

Creating this book has been a truly incredible journey and I hope that you find it enjoyable, thought provoking and that it helps you uncover your true strengths and ability.

Connect with me on instagram @thrivebythought or via my website: www.thrivebythought.co.uk. If you're a podcast fan, check out the podcast found by searching Thrive by Thought.

# Jamie's Conversation

If you had asked me a few years ago if I had a good sense of self-worth, if I felt worthy, if I liked myself, I would have said, "Yes, of course, I do."

Because, that's what you say right?

You give the answers that people want to hear. You give the answers that are safe. You tell them everything is "going great" and you're "doing just fine, thanks".

It's less complicated that way. And to be quite frank, it would have been awfully embarrassing to admit that things actually weren't going great on the inside!

The actual truth is I felt totally lost.

I felt anxious, unworthy, and I worried that I wasn't enough. I was swamped under the pressure of wanting to be better, full of ambition with a desire to succeed. The result was that I struggled to accept myself as I was. Instead I was fixated on trying to keep up with the rest of the world and to exceed the high expectations that I had for myself.

My mental health fluctuated. I had OK days, and then I had days I felt completely worthless, self-conscious and had panic attacks daily. However, on the outside, I looked happy and carefree.

I pushed on regardless, desperate to shape myself into something more worthy. I needed to be smarter, slimmer, more successful, better looking, more intelligent, more likeable, more fun, more wanted, more and more and more. Because then, and only then, would I be enough.

Self doubt was such a big part of my life, I really wasn't very kind to myself. I was constantly asking myself ... What is wrong with me?! On the outside no one would have ever expected to me to feel this way, I had a great job, great friends, lots to be proud of in my life and always seemed happy.

A lot of people feel this way.

What I was thinking and experiencing was not rare, a lot of people go through phases like this in their life, especially in their 20's when they are figuring out who they are and what they are doing with their lives. It doesn't mean there is something wrong with you, it just means you are still finding your way. The mindset I was living in was the total opposite of self-worth, self-love and self-acceptance, I didn't realise this at the time, but it was self-sabotage that sent my mental health on a roller coaster.

Over the next few years I had to work hard - really hard, to understand how to be nicer to myself, to value myself and lift myself up rather than pull myself down. It really is a journey. However, I totally shifted how I treat myself, how I connect with myself and how I view myself. Over the next few pages I will be sharing how I did this. I changed my relationship with myself and the result was amazing.

It really has been the best thing I have ever done.

Your relationship with yourself can be transformed at any point in your life, regardless of where it currently is.

I have realised how much I underestimated myself, I was doing so much better and worth so much more than I ever realised. The problem was never me, rather, the problem was how I perceived and treated myself.

Maybe there's some lesson in this for you too?

I'm pretty sure you are doing a thousand times better than you think, you are more capable than you think, more worthy than you think. Your problem isn't you, the problem is really with what you tell yourself and how you treat yourself.

This chapter is dedicated to self-worth, self-acceptance and self-love. It is a reminder that you are enough, that you always have been and always will be. A reminder that you need to take ownership of your relationship with yourself and craft a relationship full of self-love and self-worth.

Now I really like who I am and who I am becoming. In fact, I absolutely love it. I know for a fact that everything can change if you put the time in for yourself.

## What is Self-worth and Why Does it Matter?

Your relationship with self-worth is ultimately the relationship you have with yourself. It is the most important relationship you will ever have because you are the one constant in your life.

Self-worth is about seeing and knowing your true value regardless of anything else. It's about taking care of yourself, providing to your needs - emotional, physical and spiritual. It is about being kind to yourself, having respect for yourself and accepting yourself for who you are and not who you are not.

I've come to realise, self worth sits across a spectrum; it isn't a black or white, yes or no, kind of thing. It is more complex than that.

You can have high points, low points and everything in between. Your self-worth depends on how you choose to evaluate yourself and how your react to things throughout your life. Through my journey of understanding and discovering self-worth, I have come to understand that healthy self-worth is about **unconditional** love, respect and acceptance for yourself.

The most important word in that sentence is *unconditional.* An unconditional commitment to have love for yourself, regardless of anything, without conditions, no matter what.

It is about having respect for yourself no matter how others view you, how you look, what you weigh, your successes or your failures. This is what I struggled with the most, the idea that I could be good enough regardless of how the outside world judged me.

Unconditional love sounds like an impossible task but actually, everyone is fully capable of unconditional love. For example, we love our family, siblings, parents, children and spouses unconditionally. Regardless of what they do, how they behave, or even how hard we fall out with them we still have this permanent love and compassion for them.

Yet when it comes to how we love ourselves we are so much harsher. One false move and that's it. We judge ourselves. We get overly critical and question our own worth.

## Perfectly Imperfect

Looking back on my journey to self-acceptance, I now understand that a huge cause of my problem was the misconception I had. I thought I needed to be perfect.

George Fisher once said, "When you aim for perfection, you discover it's a moving target." This sums the issue up fully - self-acceptance becomes an issue for us when we strive for a level of perfection that doesn't actually exist.

Often without realising it, we take a look at the world and cultivate our own set of impossible 'idyllic' standards that we need to reach in order to be accepted by ourselves and deemed worthy. We then label ourselves as inadequate if we don't quite reach these ideals.

It may sound something like this:

**I need to:**

- Weigh a certain amount
- Look a certain way
- Achieve a certain salary
- Have a certain lifestyle
- Be seen a certain way by my peers
- Impress certain people
- Have a certain status
- Have a certain personality

**And only then will I be good enough.**

Does this resonate at all?

It resonates with how I felt so much, I felt like I had to tick off a list of achievements in order to be good enough. I now realise that in reality, no tick list or criteria actually existed for me to fulfil - I was holding myself accountable to something that was completely made up!

How often do you allow yourself to believe that if certain parts of your life were different, that alone would make you happy?

What criteria do you set for yourself?

I find that we each decide upon a set of ideals of how we should be and force ourselves to adhere to them - we then berate ourselves when they don't make us mind-blowingly happy, or if we don't achieve them.

As much as it's important to know what determines your self-worth, it's just as important to know what doesn't determine your self-worth. You are not your weight, you are not your job, your age, gender, disability, ability, or achievements. You are not your partner, salary, your parents or your past. Yet we struggle to accept ourselves fully because there are things on this list (and more) that don't fit into our definition of 'perfect' or 'enough'. As soon as I realised that none of these elements contributed in any way to my worth, I could finally start to accept myself just as I was and flourish.

Your actual worth has nothing to do with outside factors. Your worth is always there, it is a constant. However, we choose to see it as something that fluctuates depending on our performance and how we are viewed by the rest of the world.

I want to be clear. Self-worth is not about giving up aspirations of improving yourself, or accepting situations you don't like and standing still - in fact my ambition and motivation flourished as my self worth grew - I wanted more for myself then ever. It is accepting yourself for who you are right now and knowing your worth despite your supposed flaws and imperfections. It's about letting go of the need to judge yourself so harshly. It's about understanding that we are all works in progress and treating ourselves with the self-respect we deserve.

There is no perfect criteria to adhere to; chasing perfection is like dedicating your life to unicorn hunting. You are going to spend a lot of time searching for this mythical beast that doesn't exist and eventually look back on your life and wonder why you ever wasted so much time on it.

The truth is, things go wrong, you will mess up, sometimes you will fail, you will face rejection, you will be judged, you will have moments when you don't think you can do it. You will have moments of doubt, discomfort and low self-esteem.

And this is all totally OK.

Because when you commit to unconditionally loving yourself, even when it gets really ugly, you can pull through anything. You will find the light at the end of the tunnel, you will build up your confidence, you will celebrate your wins, and stop being so harsh on your 'failings'. You will stop the self-judgment and have a sense of compassion for yourself that helps you heal and grow.

## Comparison is the Opposite of Self-Love

One of the quickest ways to boost the way you feel about yourself is to stop comparing yourself to others. A huge contributing factor to our struggles with self-worth is the fact that we constantly compare ourselves to others, and as a result convince ourselves that we are lacking in some way.

I cannot tell you how many times I have scrolled down my Instagram feed and made a mental note to lose 3 stone, get a personality transplant, earn more money, go on more holidays, upgrade my wardrobe and basically be anyone but me.

Comparison is like a drug, it is addictive and no good can come out of it.

Too easily we get caught up in the world of measuring ourselves against what we perceive are other people's successes. All of this can only conclude in one train of thought. Which is "I'm not good enough" and off you go onto the emotional treadmill, pressuring yourself to be more, do more, say more, achieve more, and have more.

The reality is, our comparisons aren't even accurate! We compare our whole life (the good and bad) against the perfect and filtered parts of everyone else's lives. People only share the great parts of their life, which are often embellished to cover up the struggles and insecurities that they are actually going through. They choose not to mention their failed relationships, panic attacks in the work bathroom, whopper credit card debt, stretch marks and the fact that they feel lonely most of the time and so we assume that they are perfect and that we are broken for not being perfect.

I have learnt that what someone else is doing bares no reflection upon you and neither is it any of your business. We are all equal, we all win and lose sometimes. No one is ahead and no one is behind, and even if they were it wouldn't matter. Your life is your life, it's your journey, and all you need to focus on is you.

## Individuality Is Important

I used to hate how different I thought I was. I felt like the odd one out, the one who didn't fit, and not fitting in was bad… right? Oh how wrong I was!

We need to start embracing what makes us different.

The best part of each of us is that we are all individuals. We were blessed with individuality and so we need to stop trying to be like anyone else.

During a TED Talk in 2011, Mel Robbins shared that the likelihood of you being born as you has the odds of about one in 400 trillion. This is the probability of you being born at the time you were born to your particular parents, with your particular genetic makeup. To put that into context, the odds of winning the lottery in the UK are only 1 in 45 million. If you managed to win the lottery by hitting those odds, you would feel pretty blessed. The reality is you've already beaten much bigger odds.

On top of that your imperfections make you even more incredible. In Japan they have the term 'Kint-su-kuroi' which means 'to repair with gold'. The idea is that when a piece of pottery breaks, they repair it with gold which acts like glue. Each piece of repaired pottery has unique imperfections which makes the piece even more beautiful, desirable and rare - a one of a kind.

Everything that makes you different, every quirk, every opinion, every scar, is like a brush stroke to a masterpiece. If you start looking at things with a different perspective, maybe those flaws aren't as bad as you think. If you are still really focused on changing something, then why not look at it as a 'work in progress' instead of a failure.

## You Will Not Fit in Everywhere

I've always felt as though I had the type of personality that wasn't quite right. Growing up I was often seen as too loud or too energetic, talkative, too much. Somehow, no matter what I did, I just didn't quite fit in. I took this too personally, and as a result I doubted myself and my worth.

Personalities are so very, very personal, and when your personality is called into question it is easy to start self-sabotaging and wondering if there is something wrong with you. I concluded that there was **absolutely** something wrong with me and that **I** was the issue. I tried to change my personality in order to fit in more. I tried to be less energetic, more introverted and quieter. The end result was the opposite of what I wanted. I felt worse! It wasn't who I was meant to be - I was against my natural flow. It was forced, inauthentic and made me more miserable!

Amongst us humans, there's a myth that we need the approval of the outside world in order to approve of ourselves.

You are who you are and trying to gain approval from anyone or anything else will never give you joy. There is absolutely nothing wrong with doing your own thing. The most refreshing thing you can learn to accept is the fact that **you will not fit in everywhere**, and that is totally fine. The need for someone else's approval is exhausting and largely out of your control.

At some point along my journey, I surrendered and accepted that my personality was not going to suit everyone and **that was fine.** The main thing is that my personality suits me, and it's that same outrageous personality that led me to create this book. It lets me talk to audiences on boosting their mental wellness and contribute to the world in my own way. As a result, I found my tribe, the people who embraced me, understood me and allowed me to remain authentic to myself.

Over your lifetime you will see multiple versions of yourself and your personality as you grow, develop and experience new things. Accept that you will change, you will outgrow some environments and also fit into new ones that you never thought you would. Not fitting in is totally normal at multiple points in life. It might mean you just haven't found your place or people yet, but you will.

## Self-love Isn't Selfish

I used to think that it was selfish, self-absorbed and cheesy to pursue a path of self-love, but it is not. Now, I finally appreciate self-love, and I spoil myself rotten. I look after myself really well, as I know how essential self-love is. You are entitled to and worthy of love, support, happiness and joy. Give yourself permission to look after yourself the same way you would look after someone else in your life.

Self-love doesn't need to be done with huge gestures. It can be small things that make you feel good. I once had a colleague who would, without fail, once a week, go and get her hair blow-dried so it looked big, bouncy, and fabulous. She did this for no other reason than that it made her feel great and she decided that she deserved that! I was always in awe of someone having that much self-respect. It's about putting yourself on the pedestal you deserve.

My idea of self-love is running a hot bubble bath and loading it with essential oils and bath bombs, with scented candles everywhere. It is my therapy. It literally transforms and soothes my soul.

There are so many ways you can practice self-love and care easily and cheaply. I come up with new ones all the time. Most recently I bought myself a Fit Bit and I make a point of walking through Regent's Park to work every day. It takes me an hour but it's an hour of walking through the beautiful grounds of Regent's Park. I soak in the greenery and declutter my mind. It costs me nothing and gives me so much.

Give yourself permission to do what you need to do to get where you need to go. Allow yourself to have aspirations and goals and to think about what you would really like to experience in life. Nourish your mind and soul and know that it's your right to do so, it's really the basis of finding true fulfilment in life.

Speak kindly to yourself, quiet the inner critic and let yourself feel good.

## Act Like You Own the Joint

Some of the most incredible people I have met are not actually perfect at all – far from it. What really amazed me about them is their confidence. They just completely and utterly respected themselves. Not in an arrogant way. Instead, they were humble and confident, they knew what they were capable of. They knew they were worthy and they totally embraced themselves.

You must have met people like this too, haven't you? People who were just super comfortable in themselves. You can't help but be in awe of people like this. They are truly free. They won't let people treat them in a way that doesn't make them feel good and they do not make excuses for who they are. They just own it, flaws included!

As I have gradually built up my self-worth, I allowed myself to grow as a person. I push myself. If I want something, I go after it. I speak at events. I have built my brand dedicated to helping people create better mental wellness. I am starting my podcast and I founded this book collaboration. All because I changed my relationship with myself.

You have everything you need, and you are everything you need. It's time to start playing to your strengths. What are you really great at? What parts of yourself do you really love?

Big leaps come from small steps. Start getting grateful for who you are and what you have. Take time out to list the things that you really love about yourself that make you you. Celebrate your successes regardless of how big or small. Every single victory counts, and every failure is simply a chance to learn.

You have overcome so much, and you will overcome so much more. Your personality is incredible regardless of whether you are the loudest or quietest person in the room. You are amazing. You were designed perfectly; your flaws are beautiful.

When you start to realise that everyone in the world is equal, you will begin to realise that also includes you. You have every right to sit at the table and feel valued, loved, and respected.

## The Way we Treat Ourselves is What Matters Most

I am known for my lack of patience, and I learnt the hard way that self-acceptance isn't something that happens overnight! It's a gradual process that needs to be worked on every day.

Self-worth CAN BE BUILT, just like it can be diminished.

It took continuous effort to get to the point where I love myself for who I am. Sometimes, it felt like two steps forward and three back! I feel like I am there now. I embrace my quirky personality, my weird and wonderful mind, and I let myself run free! I know what I really love about myself. I've stopped sweating the small stuff. I've stopped listening to other people's judgement.

Of course, I have doubt days - that's what makes me human - but for every unaccepting thought there are 10 accepting ones pushing back. I have made a commitment to putting myself and my happiness as a priority. For me, self-love is not an option. It is an essential part of my happiness, health and success. Anyone can do it.

"You Alone Are Enough. You Have Nothing to Prove to Anybody"-
Maya Angelou

## You Can Do This

There are very few things we can control in life. But how we perceive and treat ourselves is something we have total control over, and the impact is literally life changing.

Self-worth and self-acceptance is a commitment to yourself to work with yourself not against yourself. People will come and go in your life, and things in life are not always smooth sailing. The relationship you have with yourself is the only constant relationship you will have forever. Looking after yourself needs to be a priority. Start supporting yourself to do the amazing things you believe you are meant to do. Be the truly amazing person you were meant to be. It doesn't matter where you have been, it only matters where you are now and where you are going.

# CHAPTER 8

# BUILDING UNSTOPPABLE CONFIDENCE

## By Twyla

I'm Twyla and I'm a female entrepreneur based in Calgary, Alberta Canada. For as long as I can remember, I've been interested in personal development, self discovery, why we are the way we are and why we act the way we act. I'm the Co-Founder of a tech company as well as the Co-Founder of an accounting firm… two industries historically led by men. I'm also the mother of a 12-year-old daughter on the Autism Spectrum who doesn't always have her own voice or the ability to communicate with the world she lives in. All of this has led me to feeling inspired to empower others to go on their own journey to discover their own unique voice. On my own life path I've discovered that the greatest gift we can give ourselves, our families, and our communities is to have an authentic belief in our abilities. This powerful tool is also known as confidence.

In 2019 I rolled out the Video per Day Experiment and had the opportunity to mentor an inspiring group of individuals who want to discover their best selves. I'm excited to be launching the Year of 30 Day Experiments in 2020.

# Twyla's Conversation

In early 2019, I found myself on a women's panel event that was being broadcast live on the internet all around the globe.

Leading up to the event, I spent time preparing because I knew I would be nervous. It was my first time doing anything like this. I was going to be part of the global stage in my professional industry and I wanted to do a good job; the only way I was going to combat the nerves was to be prepared. Or so I thought.

Despite my preparation, I was more nervous than ever I anticipated I would be. With the camera on and the entire world watching (ok the entire world wasn't watching but it felt that way) my results were mediocre compared to my desired outcome.

I kept looking away from the camera, I used a lot of filler words such as "ummm" and "like", I was shaking like a leaf and really hoping that the viewers didn't notice, and I even lost my train of thought part way through an answer. If the words "cut, let's start that over" were available to me, I definitely would have used them. But, that option was not available. This event was live and as they say in show business, "the show must go on".

After the broadcast ended, I immediately felt like hiding for the rest of the day. I really felt like I had blown it and was so incredibly disappointed in the results of the panel.

This got me thinking, what would I do if an opportunity like this arose again?

I had two choices. I could avoid the embarrassment of experiencing this all over again by politely saying "no thank you" to any future opportunities like this. Or, I could rise to the occasion, build up my confidence and figure out how I could get better.

So I chose the latter.

My confidence, or lack of, had gotten the better of me this time around. I was adamant it wouldn't happen again. I chose to face my relationship with confidence and see what impact I could make.

Confidence is an incredibly powerful force. More powerful than most of us actually realize. When confidence exists, it can enable us to take action in a way that is spontaneous, without overthinking.

The lack of confidence however can typically lead us to one of two outcomes:

1) We don't take action at all, we're not interested, and uncomfortable ideas are shut down.
2) We overthink and give far more thought than would be given if confidence were present, often with results that are subpar to our desired outcome.

I've never really given my level of confidence a whole lot of thought until that panel event. After some consideration, I realized that I've never really been an overconfident person. In fact, from my teenage years to being an adult, I recall times where I've definitely held myself back and created excuses as to why I haven't done something or haven't succeeded at levels that others have.

I've silently and verbally said "no" to opportunities that have been right in front of me... because I lacked confidence. Sound familiar?

## What is Confidence?

If I were to define confidence, I would say it's a feeling of self-assurance. An authentic belief of one's own abilities and qualities. It's about being clear on the value you bring to the world and believing that you're fully capable of doing what you've set out to do. When I'm confident, I feel like I'm unshakeable. With the belief that I can handle all circumstances, nothing is insurmountable, and the rest of the world doesn't really matter.

Confidence is an on-going endeavor. It's a work in progress and something that we continually strive for. Life, people, and circumstances will all test your confidence, but ultimately it is within our power to build or breakdown our own confidence. You're in the driver's seat and your job is to continue to strive for that clarity around the value you bring and your belief in yourself that you're fully capable.

Because, you are!

Whilst I was writing this chapter, somebody asked me what I would tell my daughter about confidence as she gets older?

Oh wow... well, my daughter has autism, and truth be told, at her young age, she's taught me a thing or two about confidence. Often, individuals with autism have no regard for what other people think about them and they'll often jump in and try something that they're not ready for. They believe in their own abilities because they don't have any reason not to. This is my daughter to a T.

So what I would like her to know about confidence is this: Don't change. Stay exactly as you are. Always continue to believe in yourself and walk into a room being brave and authentically being who you really are. This is advice we could all benefit from, not just my daughter.

## Get in The Game!

Truth be told, I loved being on the internet panel, despite how incredibly nervous I was. I loved having the opportunity to share my thoughts and ideas around a subject that I'm truly passionate about. I wanted to do it again.

In fact, I once thought I wanted to be a public speaker and deliver motivating messages until I let that dream go because it seemed too far out of reach. But this time the voice inside my head told me to get in the game. And if I was going to do this, I knew for sure that next time I wanted results that I could be proud of. Which only meant one thing: I needed to get better.

The day following the event, I set down this betterment path and put myself into my own personal challenge. I called the challenge the 'One Video per Day Experiment'. It was simple and something I could start immediately, before I talked myself out of it using familiar excuses like "I'm too busy" or "I'm not prepared enough".

Every day for thirty days, I would record one one-minute video and post it on the internet. The videos could be about anything, with no pressure to speak to a certain topic or deliver a particular message. My only hard and fast rule with this experiment was to commit to posting every single day. I was nervous, fearful, excited and apprehensive all at the same time. I'm an introvert and this is NOT something I would willingly do, but I had an objective and that objective was to become more comfortable in front of the camera.

So it began. Day one, day two, day three, posting a video each day. By day five I started to get glimpses of what this challenge was going to really teach me. Midway through, I began pushing myself as I started to feel more natural recording my videos each day. And much to my surprise, this experiment really evolved into so much more than I anticipated. Did I gain more confidence in front of the camera? Absolutely!

That was actually the predicted outcome. One would assume that after 30 days of being on camera even for just one minute per day, a higher level of comfort should naturally evolve. And it did. But the journey ended up being filled with so much more in the exploration of confidence and less about the original goal of gaining comfort in front of the camera. It turned into a discovery in confidence.

## Valid Invalid Excuses

Within a few days of starting to record my videos, there were people that I had never met reaching out to me with comments such as "these videos are easy for you because you're smart" or "you can go on the camera because you are attractive" or "I could never do these videos because I don't have the skills." Reading these comments, I realized that we often consider other people, the people who we view as 'confident people' as different from us.

We assume confident people have got something that we don't have. In fact, for years I've believed this as well. I've actually been creating what I now call 'valid invalid excuses' as to why I can't do something or why I haven't achieved a goal.

Excuses such as "I can't do that because I'm not outgoing enough", or "I can't do that because I don't have the experience". I was doubting my own abilities and created excuses that I truly believed to be valid reasons why I haven't achieved something or even why I shouldn't even try to do something. Have you ever convinced yourself that that these types of excuses are real? Often, we can't even fathom the idea that these excuses are quite simply that: excuses.

Let's acknowledge that these excuses are getting in our way, and they are 100% contributing to our level of confidence. So the sooner we can get these excuses out of the way, the sooner we can grow to the level of confidence that we desire.

## Recognizing Where You Are Currently At

Knowing that we are often guilty of creating 'valid invalid excuses', let's first consider where you are currently at, and let's begin to do that by answering these questions:

1) Can you think of a time when you turned down an amazing opportunity because you thought you weren't good enough?

2) Do you have a habit of neglecting to start something that is important to you because you felt you weren't perfect at it yet? Or felt that you lacked preparation? Or talent? Or experience?

3) Have you ever looked at someone else's ability or skill and thought "I wish I could do that"?

If you answered 'yes' to any one of these questions, you may be letting your thoughts get in your way. So this is me telling you, as your friend, get rid of the excuses.

## Dispelling the Myth

As I continued on my 30-day journey, with the decision to stop making valid invalid excuses, I then started to do more exploration into the people that I look up to. The people that exemplify a level of confidence that I want to have. I also asked my viewers to submit their perception of traits or characteristics of the people that they define as confident people. The results were quite interesting, presented in a word cloud (figure 1).

**Figure 1**

Do you know what was the most interesting thing that came from this exercise?

Not one thing came up here that doesn't already exist inside of each and every one of us in some capacity. Authenticity, resilience, courage, humility, strength, vulnerability… there's nothing that you and I don't already have inside of us somewhere.

Do these characteristics come out at certain times more than others? Sure, but these things are all somewhere deep inside of you and me!

So if confident people are just like you and me, why then do they still seem different or why does it feel like they're on another level?

Let me tell you what I now know... confident people simply have stronger 'confidence muscles'. These confidence muscles are just like any other muscle in our body—they need to be exercised and used if we want them to get strong. Confidence can be built by anyone who wants to build it. The confident person that we look at and think "wow, look at their ability" has focused and developed strong muscles in these areas of confidence. These muscles are skills that have been developed over time.

I'm likely not the first to tell you this, but it was so impactful for me to figure this out that I just want to share it with you. Confident people are regular human beings like you and I. They're normal people. They don't have super powers. Confident people have simply pushed themselves outside of their comfort zone and continue to regularly exercise their confidence muscles.

## Getting Comfortably Uncomfortable

Now the fair question to ask... 'how the heck do we strengthen our confidence muscles?'. Believe me when I tell that I've read what feels like a million books on motivation, goal achievement and gaining more confidence. I've been to conferences, listened to world renowned speakers, subscribed to blogs, taken courses, watched TedTalks... and they've nearly all come back to one underlying theory: **Get outside of your comfort zone.**

When we consider confidence, or our lack thereof, how does this apply? We already know we need to train to build our confidence and we know that we need to get uncomfortable in order to exert ourselves enough. Getting uncomfortable doesn't come naturally and often even taking the smallest steps that we know we need to take in order to get to the bigger goal can feel too uncomfortable or audacious to tackle on a regular enough basis to have an impact. It can feel overwhelming and daunting if we don't know where to start or have a realistic action plan that we can execute.

So where on earth do we start? Consider this analogy. Let's say we decide that we want to run a marathon. We haven't been running or even been a runner in the past, but we look at other runners and see their strength, their endurance, their motivation, their commitment to training and we decide we want to achieve that same goal.

We know, however, that we can't decide today that we are going to successfully run a marathon this coming Sunday. We know that running a marathon is a big goal and that we need to take steps to get there. Which means that instead of this Sunday, we set our marathon-run date in the future, far enough out on the calendar that we have time to prepare and train.

Once the date is set, then we create a clear action plan to get ourselves to the goal. Perhaps we start by coming up with a formal training schedule where we increase our mileage, ensure we have rest days and times to stretch to prevent injury. Maybe we buy some new running shoes, and download some upbeat music to listen to on our runs. We find ourselves a running partner or a running club to train with. We begin to execute a plan that starts to put one foot in front of the other each day in order to work towards the 26.2-mile goal.

Essentially what we've done is we've set ourselves up for a much greater likelihood of success. We've taken steps to make the goal of running a marathon more palatable, giving us an action plan that we can follow through on, knowing that each day's 'training' is working towards the goal. We're getting 'comfortably uncomfortable'.

Something as simple as wearing a favourite shirt that I feel really good in while I'm taking on something that is uncomfortable improves the experience. Try and make the uncomfortable moments as comfortable as possible by intertwining it with something you are passionate about, or that you love. From the one video per day experiment, I learned that the more creative we can be when it comes to bringing our goals down to a level that's more comfortable, the more likely they are to sit in a place that's not only more palatable but also more motivating and in turn very gratifying.

## Be Your Own Biggest Cheerleader

Another big lesson from the video per day experiment that I'm excited to share with you is the idea of being your own biggest cheerleader. Now that we know that confident individuals are real people like you and me, one other distinguishing facts about them is that they already believe in themselves. They challenge themselves and then believe that they are fully capable of achievement. When you think about it, if YOU don't believe in yourself or your skill level, why would anyone else believe in it? Confidence is not something that you look to others for or that you need anyone's permission to be. It's inside of you.

So what is that voice inside your head telling you? You know the one. The one that reminds you that you that you're not smart enough or good enough or talented enough. Do you hear it? If you are the one that is constantly doubting yourself, how do you expect anyone else to believe in you?

Have you ever heard the advice to talk to yourself the way you would talk to a good friend? Someone gave me that advice a number of years ago and it hit me square in the face when I heard it! If you had a friend come to you and tell you that they would like to apply for a promotion at work or take their doctorate in neuropsychology or become a public speaker with audiences in the 1,000's… would you tell your friend to stop dreaming and get a grip on reality? Or to think smaller because they don't have the skills or the ability that it takes to do these things? Of course you wouldn't! Your response would be something more like "That's great! And I'm here to support you in whatever way I can."

So what if we were to talk to ourselves like that? When we think about our biggest dreams and goals that currently feel out of reach, let's talk to ourselves like we would a friend. Encouraging ourselves to think big and support ourselves throughout the journey.

## Comfortably Uncomfortable in Action

At day 15 of my journey, I took a leap of faith. As I felt myself starting to get more confident in front of the camera I decided to up the challenge and on that very day I announced on video that I would sing, yes sing, at the end of the 30 days. Now let me tell you, I am **NOT** a good singer and even my own family had never really heard me sing. I decided that during the experiment I had a once-in-a-lifetime opportunity to really make this an experiment and I wanted to take full advantage of it.

I was nervous about singing. I hardly slept a wink the night that I announced that my singing goal because I knew that this challenge was now so much bigger. I had raised the bar to a level that was now very far outside of my comfort zone. So right within my 30-day challenge, I had the opportunity to put my theory to the test. I needed to think about what I could do to set myself up for success. I came up with my action plan and got creative around how I was going to achieve the goal of singing in front of the camera in 15 short days.

I engaged a local artist to assist me with the music as well as with my vocal pitch. I chose a song that meant something to me and aligned with my learnings from the challenge, I blocked some time in my busy schedule as a mom, wife, and an entrepreneur to practice as much as my life would allow and I arranged to record my singing video in the morning (my favourite time of the day). Let me assure you, all of these things contributed to me pulling off that video.

I did it! I sang on camera! I consciously executed ways to get comfortably uncomfortable and it worked out better than I could have hoped. Was I still nervous? Absolutely! But am I proud of the result and the video that ended up having thousands of views? Yes, I certainly am!

After little old introverted me sang on camera, it really hit me. Confidence is not a skill that is reserved for extroverts. Having confidence does not mean that you need to be the loudest one in the room or the one that's always commanding attention. Anyone can have confidence. Because having confidence is having clarity on the value you bring to the world and believing that you're fully capable of doing what you've set out to do. Which is exactly what I did. And it's what I believe you can do, too.

# CHAPTER 9

# DEVELOPING YOUR OWN IDENTITY

## By Malaika

My name is Malaika and I am a healthcare professional. Some of the authors in this book are mentors or life coaches, but my advice purely comes from my personal experiences. Hopefully that makes it relatable for you.

Working in the NHS has toughened me up and given me experiences which have helped shaped who I am. I used to be shy and very lost until I began my studies and career. I had to step up and grow myself in order to deal with intense experiences at work, things like treating heroin addicts and witnessing heart attacks; it put my whole life into perspective and helped me shape who I am and showed me what I can handle.

I manage a team of 6 people, all twice my age, which often frustrates them that they need to listen to someone so much younger. Having to take this all on has given me the confidence to be able to open up about my life.

I have a fairly normal life. Going out on the weekends to blow off some steam, spending too much on eating out, Instagramming stuff that I think looks cool! On the outside I'm no different from anyone else who may read this book, which is why I felt it was important to share my story - to connect on a deeper level and hopefully inspire you in some way.

Looking back, I would tell my younger self to stop being so scared of the future! There is nothing to worry about. You'll turn into a badass that follows her dreams no matter what people say, whilst maintaining an endearing, care-free vibe. Worrying gets you nowhere, kid! Enjoy every minute of your life.

If you want to connect drop an email to 1malaika.aziz@gmail.com

# Malaika's Conversation

### British or Asian? An Age-Old Culture Clash

It's 2019. London is saturated with people from all over the world of different religions, ages and sexualities. It is one of the most developed, accepting, and open cities where people can truly be themselves. We have cafes dedicated to cat lovers, vibrant soho gay bars, and restaurants that only serve cereal!

I am 27 years old and the first generation in my family to be raised by immigrant parents in this wonderful city. I have amazing friends, a stable career, and I'm in a great relationship, yet I struggle with my identity. I'm caught between two worlds: the 21st century London that I want to live in, and the traditional Bangladeshi world that I am expected to live in.

Before we begin, I want to be clear about something. This isn't a chapter dedicated to cliché spiel about how hard it is to be a British Asian. Nor am I here to tell you a story of wanting to focus on my happiness whilst my parents wanted me to look for a suitor, learn to be the perfect housewife, and simultaneously succeed in my career.

I want to talk to you about your identity. Your relationship with who you are. Who you identify as, and whether that is who you show up as in your life. I want to talk with you about the difficulties, obstacles and importance of the relationship we have with ourselves. Despite it sounding simple, one of the hardest things to do is to be yourself.

This chapter is dedicated to finding who you are despite the challenges, and to slay at life in your own way.

To begin, let's get all the usual identity problems out the way shall we?

1) I was raised by religious parents, but I am not religious at all and live by my own personal beliefs. Religion just isn't for me.

2) Although I am in a happy relationship, I've had to keep it a secret from my family. They won't approve of my partner because he is not Muslim.

3) I wear things that aren't considered 'modest' in my community, but funnily are considered too modest for the rest of the country.

In summary, I live a double life: The person I am, and the person I pretend to be - just like the majority of young British Asians! It is so common we even bond over it, we have a mutual understanding of how we have to lie to our parents about EVERYTHING, even though we are almost in our 30's. All jokes aside, this isn't a way to live, and it is the total opposite of owning your identity.

There are many ways we can feel lost in our own identity, and not just culturally. For some, their struggle is with their sexuality, gender, religion, race, personal beliefs, or their values. Developing a sense of personal identity is essential for our wellbeing and quality of life. However, when the person we identify as doesn't correspond with who the outside world wants us to be, we find ourselves feeling suppressed, anxious, and lost.

## The Pattern - What we Tend to Do

Those who have found themselves in a similar position seem to follow the same cycle:

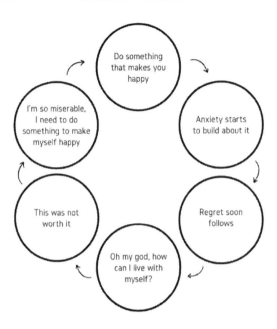

I lived in this cycle for years. I had awful anxiety issues. I almost dropped out of university because I hated my degree, but I knew my parents wouldn't approve of me studying the arts or going to culinary school. The reality is Asian parental love is NOT unconditional. That's made clear from day one.

They admit it themselves. "We love you IF...you make sure you marry someone of the same background and get a nice stable high-salary job." It's a different type of love. This kind of relationship can occur in most, if not all, cultures, meeting people's expectations can be a challenge for everyone.

So, I let myself remain in this cycle, the stress affected my health. I would force myself to live by their standards and I just got on with it. Until one morning, I woke up and thought: Is this my life now? Just getting on with it? Is that IT?!'

It was time to break the pattern.

# Epiphany

I think my turning point was finding happiness in my personal relationships. I was so terrified to try a McDonald's cheeseburger, because it was not halal, or go on a forbidden date, that I lived in a hole! Then I met someone great.

I met someone at work whom I instantly felt comfortable with. We had fun. We spoke about everything. I didn't feel judged at all. I could be my whole self, not one part of me was hidden and I loved it.

The freedom! The weight lifted off my shoulders! I actually found someone who loves me? Me. Just me, not me 'if I was a doctor' or the me that 'can be the perfect housewife'. The weirdest, loudest, sweatpants and no make-up me. You don't have to find that special someone to have an epiphany like I did. Anything can be a trigger—people, places, anything.

The main thing you have to remember whilst on a journey to finding yourself, you will have ups and downs. Although this relationship brought me happiness, not knowing who I was did affect us as a couple.

I had a lot of anger and resentment in me which I took out on him. Difficult phases in life change you. It wears away at your personality—but it's what you do with the pain that counts. You either use it to light a fire under your ass to make things better, or you let it tear you down. That's why holding on to important triggers makes a difference on your down days. Remind yourself why it made you happy in the first place and run with that feeling.

## The Importance of Your Inner Circle

Was it just my relationship that saved me? No, there was much more to it. My friends were fantastic. They supported me through all my ups and downs.

I was surrounded by amazing people who loved me. Some were experiencing the same difficulties, others weren't at all. Having a close-knit group of people from across the spectrum really opened my eyes up to the life I could have and the person I could be.

They made me feel great, they never put me down, and they were always honest when I was being a complete dick or a pushover. They were, and still are, the best friends I could ever have.

Why am I telling you about my awesome friends? **Perspective.**

Sit down and have a think about the people you surround yourself with. Do they lift you up? Are they honest, trustworthy people? Are they the kind of people you WANT to be as opposed to people dragging you down?

When you are having a difficult time, do they sugar coat things or do they straight up hit you with reality?

My friends make me feel silly sometimes, in a good way! They make me laugh when I feel like crying, and they remind me that I am much bigger than my problems. Listening to their perspective helps me to overcome my issues, so you must have people in your life that can change your perspective for the better.

You really need to assess your environment and the people you allow into your life. They need to be of the highest standard and nothing less.

What has this got to do with your identity? We all know the age old saying—show me your friends and I will tell you who you are. That shows just how important those you surround yourself with are to your identity and happiness.

## Build Your Foundations and Take Risks

So I thought I could get on with living a double life and accepting myself. And I thought I could do it by myself, without any external professional help. This of course wasn't the case.

Even with an amazing partner and friends, I had nights when I would cry myself to sleep. My anxiety constantly followed me. I would let it affect my behaviour towards my boyfriend because I was in constant fear of our messy future.

I would have nightmares about what would happen if I bought my own house and my parents came over. Where would I hide his alcohol? Would my mum find it in the cupboard while I'm at work?

I needed help and I knew it, so I turned to self-development.

Although this doesn't sound risky, it was for me.

Turning to something completely unknown, asking for help from strangers, opening up about my fears and stresses—all of it was a huge deal!

I quickly learned that it's ok to want or need help, it's okay for you to feel weak and need a companion or that extra support to get you through the day. Independence is empowering, but a part of thriving in your own life is knowing when to get help and asking the right people.

## The Wacky World of Therapy

Self-development is not widely discussed in the Asian community. Problems are ignored and brushed under the carpet. Mental health issues are still taboo. Therapy was a huge no-go. ignored all the stigma and went for it anyway.

I decided to learn about NLP. I didn't want to lie on a sofa and spill my guts out to someone and wanted to try something completely different. NLP spoke to me. It hit hard.

For those who don't know, NLP stands for Neuro-Linguistic Programming. Neuro refers to your mind, Linguistic means language, and programming is to control functions. So, in a nutshell, it is to learn about controlling the language of your mind! A huge part of NLP is perception, so you really need to be open to the ideas presented to you.

My first session was overwhelmingly intense. I loved it.

I did end up lying down on a sofa. My NLP therapist took a background of my childhood and main issues; most sessions start off with them asking you to associate certain people, feelings or memories with colours and pictures. It makes them easier to process and alter in your mind. After 2 hours of solid NLP I reached the most emotional part of my session. My therapist asked, "What do you see?"

Me: "I see myself. Slightly younger, same outfit. Skinnier, sallow complexion, tired. I look sad. Really sad. Stressed and scared. I look like a malnourished lost child."

Therapist: "What are you doing?"

Me: "Looking in the mirror. Crying. Begging for help."

Therapist: "Ask her, ask her what she wants. Comfort her, talk to her."

Me: "She wants me. She wants me to support her. She wants a hug, a friend. She wants to be loved by me, she doesn't want to feel lonely or in the dark anymore. I'm going to hug her."

Therapist: "Of course. Go ahead"

I sobbed. In my mind, the current me embraced the broken version of myself. I let her cry on my shoulder and I told her she would be okay. I told her I loved her more than anything in the world and she will always have me by her side. I told her she was going to be more than fine and that she should take care of herself. I told her to make herself a priority. She was drained because she would give her love to everyone else and left nothing for herself.

I gave myself advice. Accept myself for exactly who I am.

My parents had disapproved of my choices for all of my life. I discovered that I was doing the same thing. I was putting myself down. I was the main root of my issues and I had to stop blaming others. It was finally time for me to do something about it rather than playing the victim.

Does this resonate with you? As mentioned in other chapters, one of the most googled questions in the world is 'how can I accept myself for who I am?'

Most of you may go about your daily lives not realising how often you put yourselves down.

You build walls to protect yourself from the outside world, but how can we protect ourselves from us?

I truly believe in MIND OVER MATTER.

## From Scared to Fire Walker

That first NLP session really opened up a new world for me. It was truly the start of my self-development journey and I was so ready to take it on.

Many of you may begin by reading lots of self-help books, watching videos or documentaries online. That's fantastic, keep at it! Anything that speaks to you on a deep and meaningful level is worth your time.

I already knew my lifestyle was unique, so my approach to this journey was going to be exactly the same. I booked a 4-day intensive course—15-hour-long days of personal growth, meeting thousands of people and pretty much releasing all of the emotional baggage I had held onto. Oh, and let's not forget walking on hot fiery coals at about 2000 degrees Celsius!

It was POWERFUL. The most immersive and overwhelming experience of my life. I will hold on to all the lessons I learned, the people I met and the memories I made, forever.

I knew the path I wanted to take, but this gave me clarity. I gained a new level of confidence in dealing with my issues head on. I knew what I wanted; I didn't know how I was going to get it, but I had the utmost ambition to try my absolute best.

You don't have to walk on hot coals to have a breakthrough moment. You just have to be willing to have to be open minded to all the weird and wonderful ways there are to learn about yourself.

I truly believe that once you find a form of self development that speaks to you, it will change your LIFE!

## The Aftermath of Fire Walking and Finding Myself

The first encounter I had with my parents after this course was interesting. I told them I went on a 4-day pharmaceutical convention, so I was hesitant in telling them what I had actually done. They admired me for my bravery and communicated how they regret not focusing on their own personal mental health issues more.

Although I told them what I did, I couldn't openly tell them why. I knew I had a long way to go, I still do now. Self-development is a progressive journey, nobody is going to nail it in one day. You have to try your best but remain patient.

Nothing worth having comes easy. Move at your own pace, but make sure you MOVE.

There were moments when I felt like the old me, but that's okay.

**Here are the keys to becoming yourself and grasping your identity.**

1) **Gain clarity with what you want.** Get yourself into a stable headspace where you know what you want. Whether it's a job, a person, a goal. ANYTHING. You must make it clear. Write it down a million times, write it in huge letters and stick it on your wall—whatever works for you! Keep it clear and to the point.

2) **You have to be persistent.** If you have a goal, a belief, a vision, follow it. Try as hard as you can to achieve it. Practice any exercises you learn from self-development books, chant your daily affirmations, write in your diary-anything that you have promised yourself you would do. Make sure you do it every single day.

3) **Gratitude is EVERYTHING.** Learning to feel grateful for the smallest things will train your mind to constantly be happy. If you find joy in the sound of the rain or the feeling of the first sip of tea in the morning, everything will have a positive impact on your life. Start off small so the big things feel like BIG THINGS! Then you won't need a new car to feel satisfaction, you might just need a cuddle.

4) **Take care of yourself.** We are all drilled with information about eating well and staying active. I know, sometimes it sucks! Like leave me alone I want to eat pizza every day and I don't care that going up the stairs makes me breathless! But, shocker, taking care of your physical health improves your mental health. It's proven, it's a fact, let's not faff about. Once you push through the initial efforts of making changes to your lifestyle, you start to feel better and it becomes a reflex to make healthy choices.

5) **Allow yourself to have bad days.** We are human, after all. Embrace every emotion you feel, just channel the energy in the right way. Turn anger into motivation or self-love into loving others. Nobody is expecting you to be happy 24/7. You are going to have lazy Sundays where you just want to stay in bed. There is absolutely nothing wrong with that. You just have to make sure that, tomorrow, you will strive to keep trying. We are capable of weird and wonderful things, explore every aspect of that!

6) **Differentiate yourself.** This is the process by which you separate your parent's emotions from your own, in a healthy way. We live most of our lives worrying about what

they think and ensuring they remain happy our lifestyle. However, in adulthood this heavily influences all decisions you make, whether it be in your career, love life etc.

Differentiating from our parents means regardless of how they react to our decisions, positive or negative, we won't be affected. You respect and acknowledge their emotions but you maintain yours.

For example, If I chose to give up my stable career to become a musician and my dad panics, it won't make me panic. I will stick to my path. The age at which you differentiate can vary depending on your culture, I know some people who saw the change by 16 and some by 50 years old. Whatever the age, work towards it so you can live your own life!

Combining the above helps to make us who we are. Accepting yourself is the most liberation you will ever feel, so work hard to get there.

## In the End, for Me it Was All About Attracting the Positive

Well, I say the 'end' but it most certainly isn't so. I still find it difficult talking to my family about who I am, admitting that I'm not the model daughter/sister they want.

It still affects my sleep once in a while. The obstacles are still there, but I can handle it like a boss! I read other people's stories. I have friends who have issues which I can't even register but I stick to my path because it is mine to take. I know no other way. I've made this commitment because I have decided who I want to be.

I felt sorry for myself because of how I was treated or what I was told. I continued to make myself a victim. It got me nowhere! The moment

I started taking responsibility for how I felt was the moment I took action to make a change and that is when life turned itself around! Through my experiences, I held on to silly comments people made and slowly turned them into my own personal truths. But that is where I take the blame.

You become your thoughts. The things you constantly think about and focus on always surface. The things you tell yourself, about yourself, slowly become reality. So be kind. Watch what you think and say. It eventually becomes the truth (especially all the positive things).

Funnily enough I began writing this chapter months ago and it was so cathartic that my whole mindset became more positive. I started to attract more positive things in my life. It was easier for me to get through my down days or issues related to family and work.

It actually inspired me to sit my mum down and talk to her about how I'm not a practicing Muslim, how I'm in a relationship and how proud I am for being me. I scared myself for years thinking that she would stop talking to me. No matter how many of my friends told me she wouldn't, I was never brave enough to do it.

She hugged me. She told me it was okay and that she understood. She said that she is on my side and will always be because I'm her daughter. All those years of stress and anxiety for what? She is the mother I always knew her to be. Yes, she is upset, not because I'm not following her standards, but because she knows my life choices will make things more difficult in the future and she only wants the best for me.

We have bonded so much since, and she is my rock. It was my journey of self-development and embracing who I am that has brought me to such a pinnacle.

# CHAPTER 10

# LIVE AUTHENTICALLY, FROM THE INSIDE OUT

## By Mani

My name is Mani. If I could, I'd tell my younger self that the most powerful guidance tool you have is your instinct. Never undervalue it. The most powerful force is love and it starts with you loving yourself and filling your cup and sharing with others from that fullness.
I have a passion to empower individuals to fall in love with themselves, connect to their truth and stand in their own power. I do this through Shamanic Energy Healing and Cognitive Hypnotherapy. Working from the heart, adopting a loving and nurturing approach, I channel the energy of love through all my drumming, singing, healing and therapy work.

I also founded 'The Veda Soul Company' which creates organic raw vegan chocolates. The products are made with unconditional love and infused with healing and the chanting of sacred mantras throughout the process and you'll find a quote in each tin and box within our product range. We want people to pause and mindfully enter the eating experience.

I write daily inspirational quotes for our social media platforms. I feel that this writing is a form of channelling because I find the messages to be relevant for my own growth and healing and the inspiration continues to flow.

I'm currently bringing both aspects of my work together and expanding our brand into the experiential space, holding Cacao ceremonies that deliver a Shamanic experience held in a sublime setting, imbibed with utmost love and passion. I am loving this journey as it unfolds and hope I can inspire others to follow the dreams in their hearts.

I'd love to hear from you, you can contact me on Instagram @vedasoulcompany or @manihirani or email at manigoingforbald@gmail.com

# Mani's Conversation

I was at a fork in the road. Taking one path allowed me to stay true and authentic to my values; the other was a betrayal of my authenticity to fit into the dynamics of a group.

In writing this chapter for you, the most pertinent message that stood out to me, clearer than any other, was to encourage you to live your life from the 'inside-out'. Perhaps what I mean by this is not immediately clear, but over the next few pages it is my goal to share with you what living from the 'inside-out', rather than from the 'outside-in' is about. It was my fork in the road which allowed me to understand what 'inside-out' really means and understand what my approach to living had really been.

Your life is not an apology, so don't live it as though it is. Let me explain.

- Do you ever have that gut feeling that something is not right with how you are living? Are you are living someone else's version of your life and you are not in the place you should be?

- Do you ever feel lost, stuck or unfulfilled?

- Do you ever find that you need to justify your decisions or what matters to you to others around you?

- Do you ever feel as though your right to be happy comes second to the happiness of others around you?

If the answer to any of these questions is 'yes,' then this is an indication that you are living your life as though it were an apology. Living life as an apology means that you have surrendered your right to live life as you choose it. You have handed your power to external forces leaving you apologizing for who you really are, how you really feel, and what you really want. The outside is dictating, defining and shaping your life, rather than what is inside you. As a result, you are living 'outside-in'. Living this way is not authentic to who we really are.

I spent 22 years working in investment banking. Investment banking gave me great experiences and opportunities for growth, so I don't regret this phase of my life. However, in the latter half of those two decades, the gut feelings that arose many times were trying to show me that this line of work was not bringing me joy nor aligning me to my life's purpose. I was constantly shutting those gut feelings down. I was living 'outside-in' during this time because I was dismissing my instincts while granting the identity and lifestyle that came with the job the power to guide me.

Living from the 'outside-in' is living in a way that is not authentic to who we really are. It's when your actions, words, decisions, lifestyle are not in line with your identity, values, beliefs and true sense of who you are.

From the day we are born, we spend our lives absorbing the beliefs that we have been shown by the outside world. As we grow, we learn to accept certain norms and values that were never really our own. It is only later that we realise that these don't always connect with who we really are. Often, you know who you are and where you want to go, but external situations, people and the path you have found yourself on, are taking over and ultimately steering you in a different direction to what you so clearly desire. It's like being a puppet, being pulled in various directions, and none of them the right one.

Living authentically is about connecting to ourselves and honouring our needs. Therefore, we must believe in ourselves and let go of the need for validation from others. Focusing on our own life is not selfish; it is basic self-care. When we honour ourselves and our needs, we create happiness. When we are filled with happiness and love, we create more of it into the world around us. Happiness, therefore, creates more happiness, but when it is withheld, resentment and bitterness arise and destroy the positivity.

Many of us are stuck in some way or another because of something that might no longer align to what is important to us. We could be stuck to a salaried job and the comforts that the salary acquires us, to the loyalty that comes with wanting to belong to a group, family or institution or to a location because convenience is more comfortable than the unknown territory that comes with change.

## Are You Gripped By Fear?

Sometimes, what we really want in our life far outweighs the salary, belonging, or the convenience, yet we are too scared to let go and reach for what we really want. This fear comes from not fully understanding the power of our own authenticity and its ability to guide us to our ultimate purpose in this lifetime. It also comes from not knowing our true self because we are constantly distracted by the noise and distraction of how we 'should' be living.

'Should' always comes from the outside world. 'Feel' and 'know' are the words of the inner world.

I have been there, too.

It's exhausting, frustrating, and it can leave you feeling like you have no control over your life. You live your life by second-guessing what others around you would want rather than through the guidance of your own heart and deepest instincts.

In the process, we are constantly shutting down our gut feelings and invalidating their guidance, and, over time, this erodes our sense of self-confidence. As a result, you might feel anxious, lost or simply unfulfilled. You know something isn't quite right, but it's hard to pinpoint exactly what it is.

The cost of living inauthentically is that you end up feeling that you are living a life that's not yours. You go into autopilot, lose interest and fulfilment. You feel the strain, you don't feel like you, and the whole time something inside you yearns to change this.

All of this hurts our mental space. It creates a feeling of hopelessness, erodes our motivation and drive for life and leaves us feeling lost, as though our life is not ours to live.

When I finally acknowledged that I was living 'out-side in', I took action. I left my banking job and set up my own business making handcrafted vegan chocolate. Setting up my business was a culmination of letting go of many more layers of conditioning picked up during the 'outside-in' living of my life.

When you can visualise your intentions and can incubate them internally without letting outside influences sway you, you can generate power beyond your imagination to create beauty beyond your visions. Until your ideas are tangible to the outside world, it can be a lonely journey, and being 'inside-out' in your focus carries you through this phase and then others begin to share and start seeing your vision, but that is never the starting point, nor the dependency. When we can take full responsibility for our life, we will be at peace because we can be authentic and fully present in our actions and our choices.

It's important to really get to know yourself. Who are you? What do you care about?

What are you drawn to? What doesn't sit right in your life currently? Where in your life are you being inauthentic? How do you want to live? What do you want?

Whilst reading these questions, you may be sensing some resistance arising within you. Pause for a moment and sit with those feelings; are they feelings of denial, shame, frustration or guilt, or are they feelings of an entirely different nature?

As awkward as this may be, it is important to feel those feelings because they are yours and feeling them is the first step towards living from the 'inside-out'. Feeling them enables you to honour them as your own. Honouring them is a form of self-respect. It is a way of valuing yourself as you deserve to be valued. It is from this place that you will be able to start your journey into living from 'inside-out.' You live a life that is authentic, connected to the core of your being, a life where you are in control and at peace with who you are and who you are becoming. When we are in control, then our actions are genuine, and we are fully engaged, connected and present to what we are incapable of feeling for ourselves.

Let go of expectations and learn to appreciate the purity of each moment and the vision of the future you want.

In my experience, switching to an 'inside-out' way of living can be difficult because of the lack of confidence we have in ourselves. While living 'outside-in' we have pushed ourselves to the sidelines for too long and trying to bring ourselves back to centre-stage is overwhelming, to say the least. Whilst we absolutely belong on centre-stage as the main star of our own show, it is a mighty feat to take lead role, having spent so much time taking orders as part of the backstage support. When we first start listening to the voice inside, doubts will arise and external forces who have become accustomed to us delivering their orders may react adversely, exacerbating our doubts further.

During the transition period your vulnerability is high and, at first, it will be difficult to trust and rely on your own feelings and needs. And you may find yourself wanting to run back to the 'comfort' and 'convenience' of being under the control of the puppet strings.

Being the focus of our own lives will initially feel uncomfortable. I am sure you can relate to that. It is a difficult yet powerful shift, but we must persevere because confidence takes time to build and intentions take time to strengthen, as you fully transition into an 'inside-out' life.

Is it time for you to embody that lead role?

We arrive in this world on our own and depart on our own. What truly counts is everything that happens in between. If the precious time between arrival and departure is spent living to someone else's desires, then we will not have truly lived nor let our own light shine into the world.

Living our fullest life does not have to be frantic in activity, but is about connecting to who we are and allowing ourselves to be from this space within ourselves. When we live authentically, we connect to who we truly are, uncovering our true purpose and our own light.

If we are too busy trying to fit in, we'll never be able to uncover our own light. We are here to shine our own ray of light and shine it bright.

If you are invited to an event and you are not comfortable about refusing the invite, despite not wanting to attend, follow the feeling of discomfort through to understand what is triggering the discomfort. It's likely that you care about what that person thinks because you need their approval or validation, or you are afraid to impact your sense of belonging to that group.

Our need for validation and approval is the expectation that forms the strings. The way the host might react when you decline the invitation is the button that controls the strings. In trying to obtain validation and approval, we dismiss our own feelings while we attend events despite not wanting to.

Reflecting upon the non-fulfillable nature of expectations, it is unlikely that your attendance will give you the validation and approval the way you expected. When we attend because we are fearful of the consequences of not attending, this is a form of self-betrayal.

Coming back to my fork-in-the-road story, a stream of hypocritical behaviour and a lack of openness in discussing areas of conflicting behaviour had begun to erode my trust in the religious organisation I had dedicated a decade of my life to.

The left-hand path coming off the fork in the road was urging me to listen to my gut feeling to realise that this was the end of the road. I could no longer be part of something that was betraying my ability to be authentic. This was my 'inside-out' path because it was asking me to honour the voice within.

The right-hand path coming off the fork in the road, was the external pressure from the group and carry on regardless. This was clearly the 'brush it under the carpet' approach, this was my 'outside-in' path.

Authenticity has always been very high on my list of personal values. Choosing which path to take was difficult because staying authentic to myself required me to go against the guidance of the elders—people I had respected for a decade. This was a major turning point in my life. Making this decision was a major challenge. After much deliberation,

I chose the left-hand path and inevitably, this chapter became a significant milestone in my life's journey.

Choosing the left-hand path was not a clear-cut conclusion, there were multiple obstacles in choosing that path. Whilst the right choice is not always the easier one, when it is made with authenticity then you can stand firmly by it, taking full responsibility for every action taken to honour that decision and to bear all the ensuing consequences.

To know our authenticity and remain grounded in our values, our relationship with ourselves needs to be strong. From this place, we can continue down our path with strength, compassion and courage, working through any dark times as they descend. When we are more present and connected within, we can honour our feelings without judging them as negative or positive. As we tune-in, we evolve deeper into awareness. And with awareness we can continue embracing the 'inside-out' way of living.

Social media is another great illustration of 'inside-out' versus 'outside-in' living. When we can post something that is important to us, purely because we feel inspired to share with our friends and followers, without being worried about the number of likes, views or comments, then this is an 'inside-out' perspective, and we are authentic in wanting to share. When we are fixated on how others perceive us through the number of likes, views and comments that our posts receive, this is an 'outside-in' perspective and takes away the authenticity of sharing.

It is when we are authentic to our own thoughts and needs, that we can interact with congruence, delivering the full magnificence of who we truly are. Living from 'inside-out' allows us to release the full potential of our creativity so that we can begin to explore the full extent of our gifts and connect to our true divine purpose.

The real-life exploration of the living 'inside-out' for me happened during the lead-up to my 40th birthday celebration. I was toying with what I wanted. Then I realised that I already had all the things that were of true importance and what resonated with me was to give back to those who didn't have the things that I was blessed to have. I decided my gift to myself would be to take 6 months off work to volunteer with 3 charities and to shave my hair to fundraise for those charities.

Of course, hair is a big part of our outer beauty and while I was determined and fully enthusiastic about my choice, what became apparent was how many people around me were feeling very uneasy about what I was about to do. The comments astounded me and made me realise how much we were attached to our hair and yet I couldn't understand why I was struggling to resonate with their resistance against what I was about to do.

There were some comments which suggested that what I was about to do was a big egotistical PR exercise. I realised then how much I had changed, how inwardly focused my thinking had become and none of these external comments, challenges or projections seemed to be registering. I knew why I was doing what I was doing and that is truly all that mattered, to justify my actions did not even remotely register as a necessity and I felt a strong commitment to my decision.

The head shave itself was a joy and a liberation on so many levels and it was in that moment that my understanding of 'inside-out' took true shape because it made me reflect on how 'outside-in' my life had been in the lead up to my entering the 5th decade of my life.

Life should be lived deliberately with joy in our hearts and happiness in our every action. Our life is not meant to be lived as though it were an apology, because it is not. We are here on earth, to live our life to its fullest and to express ourselves in the highest form that we can.

'Highest' does not mean being greater than others but being connected to our higher selves, where we choose expansion and growth over limitation and protection, where we choose to connect to love and give, instead of restricting in fear, and where we choose the path that allows us to be 'our best', not 'the best'.

Sing your own song, not the song that has been handed to you by others. Allow your melody to resonate through the universe. Shine your light and do not feel the need to hide it or tone it down because you were born to shine, and shine you must. Allow your brilliance to radiate and inspire those around you.

Be your own master and do not feel the need to reform to anything that compromises your truth. Allow your strength and courage to empower others to walk out of the prison-cells which they have confined themselves to. Give yourself permission to be your truth, to live from 'inside-out' so that those around you feel inspired to grant themselves permission to do so too.

# CHAPTER 11

# BRINGING GRATITUDE INTO YOUR LIFE

## By Shumaila

I am Shumaila. I am a transformation coach for parents, I have helped 100s of people with mindset, mental health and improving their lives and the lives of their families through my 1:1, group programs, and appearances across several platforms. Being a former teacher for a decade and now a parent I have seen the impact parents have on their child's thinking, beliefs and confidence. These make up the programs that run throughout their adult lives, affecting their health, relationships, finances and their happiness!

My mission is to raise the consciousness of parents so that they are aware of what they are passing onto their children and are questioning whether it is actually serving them and the impact it will have on their child's future. I know this would have had a huge impact on my upbringing! I believe the solution is becoming the best version of yourself and building a life you love so that you can be the best parent possible, enabling you to lead by example.

I have seen this in my personal life and lives of my clients.

I love what I do because I get to wake parents up to their potential and equip them so they can do the same for their children. I witness their happiness, inner peace, health improve and the relationship with their children flourish. Happy parents results in happy children!

If I had the opportunity to go back in time to speak to my younger self, I would tell her to focus on self-love, to prioritise her health, to question her beliefs and thinking and most importantly not to take life so seriously! I plan to leave behind a legacy that will have a ripple effect on generations to come and will positively contribute to society.

You can connect with Shumaila through email, joining her free Facebook group called Awakened Parents or sending her a message on Facebook.
Email: shumaila@shumailamahmood.com
Facebook group:
https://facebook.com/groups/614563202374982
Facebook:
https://www.facebook.com/shumaila.mahmood

# Shumaila's Conversation

**"Start each day with a positive thought and a grateful heart."** —
Roy T. Bennett, The Light in the Heart

We may all be very different, live different lives, have different goals
and are different people - but without a doubt we have one thing in
common. We all want to feel happy most of the time. It's the pursuit
of happiness that drives us to achieving our goals. At the end of the
day, regardless of the goal you are pursuing, you are ultimately seeking
to feel joy and happiness in your life.

However, consistently feeling happy can sometimes feel like a
challenge. It goes without saying that there will be times that you are
unhappy. Maybe you are struggling with your current circumstances.
Life happens, hurdles arrive, and the feeling of overwhelm can creep
in.

Whilst on my own journey of trying to manage the peaks and troughs
of my own emotions and life, I have found myself reliant on one tool
in particular that helps ground me, calm me and bring me to feel a
sense of peace. I want to share this with you throughout my chapter,
in the hope that it is something that can help you too.

You might be thinking, "Great. This tool works for you, but you don't
know what I am going through." Or, you might be saying, "You don't
know how I feel!" I am not here to belittle your life experiences or the
challenges you are currently facing. We each face our own individual
challenges. However, regardless of what is happening in my life, I find
that gratitude is the tool that helps me.

## What is Gratitude?

*'Every day, think as you wake up, today I am fortunate to be alive, I have a precious human life, I am not going to waste it.'* **Dalai Lama**

Gratitude is feeling thankful. It is a feeling of appreciation and there are no limits to what you can appreciate and be grateful for. This includes material things, people, situations and even how you feel. You have access to gratitude at all times. It costs nothing, requires no equipment and is one of the best ways to get through any challenge you experience in life.

## Why do We Need Gratitude in Our Life?

*'Gratitude opens the door to... the power, the wisdom, the creativity of the universe. You open the door through gratitude.'* **Deepak Chopra**

Gratitude is the simplest and easiest way to make you feel good. It is accessible to everyone, and you can start using it instantly!

Your mind cannot focus on two thoughts at any one time. By occupying your mind with gratitude, you are focusing on the good things that you have in your life, and this, in turn, is a gentle mood booster.

Even in one's darkest moments, it is possible to slow down and find something you are grateful for in your current position. For example, are you alive? Breathing? Heart beating and blood flowing? Are you able to read this book? Although typically we take these things for granted, and they may seem like small insignificant things, they are actually incredible gifts. They are a positive in your life, regardless of what else you are facing. We just sometimes need to change our perception to remind ourselves of this.

As a result, we can change our lives by making small changes to our thinking, making a conscious effort to think and feel positive leads to a great life. Although this sounds so simple, it can sometimes feel like hard work when we are stuck in a rut, focused on our problems or interacting with negative people and circumstances.

If you only focus on what's wrong in your life, you will magnify the negative emotions attached to that, and it becomes easy to get into a cycle of negative thinking. Negative emotions strengthen, and it makes it harder to lift your mood. Gratitude interrupts these thought patterns and encourages you to focus on your blessings, lifting your mood.

Does this solve all of your problems? No. Emotions are not as simple as that. What it does do is remind you of the good that there is in your life.

When I have been faced with challenging times in my life, gratitude has been the key ingredient that has helped me through. It has made me realise how much I have to be thankful for. Even when people have wronged me I have been able to let go and shift my perspective on life. I have recognised my growth and the lessons learned. Gratitude allows me to see the best possible action. As a result I have felt lighter, happier and more focused on the things which really matter.

On average, we have 60,000 thoughts each day, most of which are repeated. This explains why it is so easy to think negatively. This is why daily mindset work and spending time looking after your mental wellbeing is so crucial.

## How has Gratitude Helped Me?

There have been many times in my life where the journey has been really tough. A few Christmases ago, my granddad passed away. It was less than 2 months after I had my first baby. I was in pieces. It was a time in my life where I had so much to process.

143

It was difficult knowing that he had passed away. His face played over and over in my mind. I just couldn't sleep for several nights after his funeral.

I knew that, emotionally, I could very easily have spiraled out of control. It was incredibly hard to do anything but focus on the loss and ignore everything else in my life. So I took time each day to practice gratitude and it was this daily practice that got me through and kept me going when I felt I couldn't.

I was so grateful that a week before my Granddad's passing I made it to his home, despite the struggle of getting there in the snow. I remember finding the journey so difficult, but my intuition told me I had to see him.

I was so grateful that he got to hold my son in his arms, and to see him, delighted to do so.

I took time to focus the incredible life my granddad lived, and how the family came together to support each other after his passing.

Despite all this pain, I worked hard to focus on whatever positives I could find. Big or small.

Regardless of what you are feeling right now or what you are experiencing in your life, I invite you to try and be grateful. To think of any positives you have in your life.

## How to Implement Gratitude Into Your Life

*"Cultivate the habit of being grateful for every good thing that comes to you, and to give thanks continuously. And because all things have contributed to your advancement, you should include all things in your gratitude."* — **Ralph Waldo Emerson**

I often start my day very positive, optimistic, and full of energy. However, as the day goes on, and I come across challenges, things may not always go to plan and I can find myself zapped of energy. The

144

negative thoughts can start creeping back in. It is at this point I always stop myself and have a think about what I am grateful for. This always recharges my batteries, shifts my perspective, and I feel better, ready to continue the day with focus.

Many people think gratitude is far more complicated than it is. It's simply being thankful for what you have. There are many ways you can express this. You can think about it, say it out loud, make gratitude lists, write a letter of gratitude or just go on a gratitude rampage where you write out every tiny thing you are grateful for and how much it means to you. There is no right or wrong way to include gratitude in your life. The key is just to include it. Whichever way you choose you will feel the benefits.

The easiest way to incorporate gratitude into your daily life is through an already existing routine. So, for example, if you already have a morning routine, make it a part of that.

Another way to make it easy for you to stick to a habit is by creating a trigger. Think of your daily activities. For example, you could think of everything you are grateful for when you're in the shower. You could say them out loud as you are getting dressed in the morning or whilst driving to work.

Other ways you can include gratitude is by setting an alarm on your phone so you don't forget. The key is to make it as simple as possible so that it doesn't feel like another item on your to do list. That way you are more likely to stick to it and reap the benefits from it.

Every so often it's good to change things up, especially once you have made gratitude a habit. You can either express gratitude at different points in the day or set up other triggers.

You can even go the extra mile by sending people gratitude letters and gifts, really taking the time to show them how much you love and appreciate them. This can have a massive impact on your relationship and how you feel. I posted a gratitude card to my husband and the effect it had on our marriage has been profound! Give it a go. You really will feel amazing!

## How to be Grateful When you Really Don't Want To

When you are struggling and in a negative headspace, it can really be a challenge to get yourself to feel grateful in that moment.

It's important to remember that it won't always be easy! I found that my relationship with gratitude grew over time. You may think at first, "I have nothing to be grateful for." However, the more you encourage yourself to think about what makes you grateful the easier, more enjoyable and uplifting this tool can be.

## Gratitude and Mental Health

Gratitude for me has been a natural tool for me to create inner peace and stability in my mental health. Gratitude played a huge part in overcoming my anxiety a few years ago.

Gratitude creates a blank canvas for your day, it interrupts the autopilot cycle of focusing on the things that are challenging in your life or all the things that need to be done. Gratitude puts you in charge of your thoughts and emotions, which is so empowering!

*Make it a habit to tell people thank you. To express your appreciation, sincerely and without the expectation of anything in return. Truly appreciate those around you, and you'll soon find many others around you. Truly appreciate life, and you'll find that you have more of it.* - **Ralph Marston**

Now that you know the benefits of gratitude, I want to share with you how you can simply incorporate it into your life. The next step is to make a plan and put things in place so that you make it into a habit. Here are four easy steps to follow:

146

**Step 1: Decide when.** Will it be part of your morning, afternoon or evening? What daily action can you pair it with? E.g. when making breakfast, exercising or driving.

**Step 2: Decide how.** How are you going to express your gratitude? Will it involve thinking about it, saying it out loud, or writing it down?

**Step 3: Track.** Track it for at least 21 days to help you develop a habit of gratitude. It's extremely satisfying ticking it off a tracker everyday!

**Step 4: Change it up.** Every so often, include another way or an additional time to express your gratitude to ensure it doesn't feel like a chore!

# CHAPTER 12

# MINDFULNESS - A WAY TO IMPROVE YOUR MENTAL WELLBEING

## By Delia

My name is Delia Serban, I have been a practitioner for over 15 years. I discovered mindfulness, yoga and meditation in my hardest time. I am grateful I found them, because they helped me become the woman I am today.

I am a normal person and I have a normal life. I have had unhappy moments, experienced betrayals, disappointment, and grief just as everyone else does. Since I discovered mindfulness, I have learnt to reconnect with myself. I have learnt to deal with these situations without letting them affect me in they way they did before. With mindfulness I am able to remain "in the light", I manage to keep my faith in myself, to discover and love myself more than I have ever done before. I discovered mindfulness and yoga in 2005. Since then I have come across with a strong sense of spiritual purpose, positive attitude and joyfulness; a life full of transformation and personal growth.

I am a qualified yoga, wellbeing, and healthy-eating coach with a diploma in Psychology and Mindfulness. I am a healthcare professional and I have been working as a registered Pharmacy Technician in the UK for 10 years. I am dedicated to continuously improving myself and helping others to become happier and more fulfilled.

In May 2018, I published my first book called "Mindfulness- Discover Happiness Inside of You", a book where I gathered all my experience, techniques, tips, exercises, advice and meditation routines which will enable anyone at any level to follow the breath, still the mind and relax the body. The book was launched in my hometown in Romania and had great success.

In October 2019, I published my second book called "Mindfulness- A way to improve your mental wellbeing". This book can be used alongside your meditation practice, any time you want to relax your mind and body and it is for anyone at any level of practice. I hope that you enjoy discovering mindfulness and you will integrate it into your life in your own way.

I am hoping that with all my writings I will be able to send a message to you all, to make you understand that the power is with you, to be aware that your happiness depends on the way you think, talk and act, and you are the only one who determines your life.

Whatever you do in your life, don't forget to be happy and cherish your joy!

With love, Delia

# Delia's Conversation

I discovered Mindfulness, Yoga, and Meditation in my hardest time, and I am grateful I found them, because it helped me become the woman I am now.

I am a normal person, I have a normal life. I have happy moments, I have unhappy moments. I have experienced disappointments, betrayals, and have grieved just like anyone else.

Since discovering Mindfulness, I learned to reconnect with myself, I can deal with situations without letting it affect me like before. With Mindfulness I manage to remain "in the light." I manage to keep my faith in myself, to discover and love myself more than I ever had before.

I discovered Mindfulness and Yoga in 2005, and since then I have found a strong sense of spiritual purpose, positive attitude and joyfulness, a life full of transformation and personal growth. I am a qualified yoga instructor, Wellbeing and Healthy-Eating Coach. I've got a diploma in Psychology and Mindfulness. I have been a healthcare professional, working in the NHS as a registered Pharmacy Technician for 10 years. I am dedicated to continuously improving myself, helping others to become happier and more fulfilled.

Within this chapter, it is my hope to make you understand the power that is inside of you, to guide you to be aware that your happiness depends on the way that you think, you talk, you act and that you are the only one who creates your life.

We live, but we are not present in our lives. Life is busy. We all have thousands of things we should do and thousands of things we should have already done. Worries in the future, worries in the past and problems in the present.

Stress, stress, stress! Finding time to improve and prioritise our mental and physical wellbeing is not always easy.

Have you ever found yourself parking your car, only to discover that were unable to recall a single detail of the drive? Sometimes we sit down for a coffee, only to find that we are left holding the empty cup! We are performing these actions on autopilot as we are so consumed with our thoughts. Often, we are not aware of either thoughts or actions; experiences and details are lost due to distractions. The tendency to worry about several things at once interferes with our ability to focus on the present moment. As a result, we tend to function on autopilot and become 'mindless'.

## What is Mindfulness and How is it Relevant to Our Lives?

Mindfulness is the art of accessing the energy that helps you recognise the happiness that is already in your life. It helps you to silence your mind, calm your nerves, and examine your inner world. It is the practice of cultivating conscious awareness of our thoughts, feelings and environment in every moment, without judging the experiences. It is the art of focusing on the present, without being hindered by judgements. Regular practice of Mindfulness leads to an overall improvement in general wellbeing and you can look forward to leading a fuller, richer, and more fulfilling life.

Mindfulness can become your natural state, the state in which you should be living. When you become mindful, you begin to notice your life. You start to take note of all the interesting aspects of your life, whether it be in your relationships, home, or career.

This way of life can help you enjoy an improved sense of control over your reactions at any given moment. Even when you are multitasking at home or at work, the mind can only focus on one thing at a time. Our reactions or responses to a situation in our everyday lives can differ, depending on our balance on that particular day or moment. Mindfulness can be practiced anywhere, it is not limited to the silent comfort of your own home, it can be utilised effectively in the workplace, or anywhere you find yourself!

You can practice Mindfulness by simply bringing your awareness to the present moment.

Mindfulness meditation is a practical tool with which one can observe inner and outer experiences with compassion, acceptance, and neutrality. Regular and consistent meditation practice promotes calmness and inner stability while reducing impulsive and reactive behaviours.

With Mindfulness meditation we learn to separate ourselves from the flow of emotions, stress, and anxiety and to connect with our lives and with others in a more profound manner. Becoming mindful helps us to draw our focus to the present moment, to appreciate life in all its forms and qualities. The more you put this practice into action, the more it will become natural for you to live your life to the fullest.

## How to Perform Mindfulness Meditation

Choose a comfortable posture. You can choose to sit on the floor or you can sit against the wall, with your legs extended in front of you. Sit with your spine straight. Do not arch your back. If you suffer from back pain, hip, or pelvic pain, please take particular care with regard to supporting your back. You can lie down on the floor or use cushions for support.

Focus your eyes on the tip of your nose or on a stationary object. Try to relax your eye muscles and ease your emotions. Depending on what feels comfortable for you, you can keep your eyes open or closed. If your eyes are closed, imagine yourself in a safe, comfortable, serene place.

Place your palms down on your thighs, your thumb and forefinger lightly touching each other. Try to keep the rest of the fingers relaxed.

Now, focus on your breathing and become aware of the sensations and the thoughts that you are experiencing. It might be heaviness, pain, itching, lightness, or angry thoughts. Try not to attempt to analyse any of them, simply observe them and let them go. Try to observe each sensation or thought with full awareness.

Slowly come back into awareness by taking five slow, deep breaths. Breathe in through your nose, exhale through your mouth. Rub your hands together, in order to generate heat, and place your palms on your eyes. Then interlock your hands and stretch your arms above your head. Whilst maintaining the stretch, try to lean to the left and right five times. Keep this meditative moment for as long as you wish and try to carry this feeling with you for the rest of the day.

## Mindfulness is an Excellent Way to Reconnect with Yourself

Our beliefs, perceptions, and attitudes are deeply coloured by external experiences and events. Mindfulness is an excellent way to reconnect with yourself without the external stimuli. The main objective of meditation is to shift mental focus away from the worries and problems of daily life.

Our minds are often overwhelmed with worries regarding finances, relationships, health, job security, etc. Our thoughts either focus on the unknowns of the future or dwell on the past. This chaotic state of mind makes it difficult to live in the present moment.

Mindfulness interrupts thought and emotion. It observes both peak and flow as it plays itself out. Today, the benefits of Mindfulness are universally acknowledged. With Mindfulness, we learn not to become victims of regret, past resentments, or worries about our future. We are no longer at the 'mercy' of negative emotions because we learn to choose our reactions to life's challenges. We become more proactive in the face of stress and adversity.

The most important benefit of Mindfulness meditation lies in its potential to reduce stress levels. Our minds are often in a state of overstimulation. The first thing that most of us do upon waking up in the morning is to check our phone for messages, social media, work emails, etc. As we are constantly on our phones or computers, it has reached a stage whereby we cannot be still for even five minutes without some kind of technical interaction. The objective of Mindfulness is to focus on an object, our breath, a flame, a picture or even our imagination in order to become mindful.

## The Importance of Mindful Breathing

How often do we really think about our breathing? Breathing occurs so naturally that we don't necessarily have to give it much thought. Breathing only ever becomes an issue if we find it difficult in some way, then we become far more conscious.

## How to Perform Mindful Breathing

This is a very simple but powerful meditation exercise that helps one develop Mindfulness.

Sit comfortably in a chair, a mat or cushion. You can keep your legs crossed or extended in front of you. Whichever posture you choose, sit with your spine straight, do not arch your back.

Focus your attention on your breathing and become the physical act of breathing. Keep your attention focused on your inhalations. Try to observe the sensations of warmth or coolness as you breathe in. Pay attention to your lungs and notice that your diaphragm expands when you breathe in and relaxes when you breathe out. Pay attention to the sensations on your upper lip, just below your nostrils, as you breathe out.

Do not try to regulate your breathing. Simply observe how your body breathes naturally. Pay attention to the process. Your breathing could be deep or shallow, fast or slow. Pay attention to your breathing. As thoughts come and go, allow them to leave without judgement, without criticism. Slowly, continue to bring your attention back to your breathing. This exercise can be practised simply and with zero fuss. Try for five minutes at first and then gradually increase the time.

When we meditate, the first thing we notice is the sound of our own breathing. The breath is a central focus for many meditations because it is highly effective at keeping our concentration. It helps ground us in the present moment.

Mindfulness helps us perceive reality without the distortion of personal bias or emotion and to make appropriate decisions. It helps us manifest positive, empowering results due to purposeful deliberation. We often see either positive or negative results, but we remain unaware of the thoughts and actions that helped manifest those results.

We are always waiting to be happy and fulfilled. Our minds are always focused on the next minute, the next entertainment, next job, next car... and the list goes on. We are alive without being aware of it.

Most people want happiness, peace and joy in their lives; however, the mind has a tendency to get stuck in pain, anxiety and stress. The main objective of Mindfulness meditation is to shift mental focus away from the worries and problems of daily life. Mindfulness meditation trains the mind to disconnect the inner self from nagging thoughts. You must teach yourself to think in the following manner: There is that troubling thought, but it's just a thought and not a part of me. It will release itself and disappear.

Mindfulness meditation is an excellent way to revitalise the energy flows in your mind and body and elevate your energy vibration. It helps you to get in tune with your true being by releasing negativity, including feelings of frustration, anger, resentment and low self-esteem. It helps you to promote feelings of joy and confidence and become the best version of yourself.

If you are used to thinking negatively about yourself, you may initially find it challenging to change. However, through the practice of regular Mindfulness, stubborn thought patterns can be replaced with empowering thought processes. The way we think (and what we think about) can affect how we feel and act. If we think or worry a lot about upsetting past or future events, we might often feel sad or anxious.

In order to maintain a balanced, positive, healthy outlook on life, we need to release negative thoughts. We all have, at times, negative thoughts. We also tend to dwell on these thoughts of frustration, worrying over a deadline, to not having enough time to meet friends, job performance or general feelings… What we need to do is to curb negative thinking. Letting go of these thoughts, instead of holding onto them or denying them, is a way to refresh our mind.

The healing power of Mindfulness meditation lies in the fact that we are able to establish a connection with our thoughts, accept their existence and come to terms with reality. We are able to make peace with our internal experiences, instead of being driven by hatred or fear. Mindfulness meditation does not teach us to avoid pain or worry, but it empowers us by training the mind to acknowledge, accept and experience the worry or the pain. It helps us focus on the task at the present moment, regardless of the external circumstances in our lives. Awareness of our thoughts helps enhance physical and mental wellbeing and helps us enjoy whatever we do.

This chapter will help you get started with Mindfulness right now, right here, so you have the basic tools to start developing your Mindfulness practice. It's so simple...

In a world where you can be anything.... BE MINDFUL!

# CHAPTER 13

# CALMING MENTAL CHATTER

## By Claus

I wear many hats; I work as a life coach and love working with people who have started their personal development journey on their own. I can help to integrate initial breakthroughs into their life so that they never fall back to old habits and instead make lasting positive changes. I'm passionate about addressing mental chatter and mastering your thinking. I got into personal development years ago when I founded a tech startup and know how powerful it can be; I was quite sick at that time (you can read more about it in my chapter) and realised how powerful the human mind is!

I enjoy passing my knowledge on to others. It's amazing to look in someone's eyes when they just had a profound realisation and see their eyes light up like a firework. I cherish those moments!

I'd tell my younger self to be more confident and just go for it. I was so timid when I was young across all areas of my life.

Besides coaching, I work with large enterprises as a corporate consultant; I also invest into property and still love tech startups.

claus@amstadd.com

https://www.facebook.com/AmstaddCoaching/

www.amstadd.com

# Claus' Conversation

With so many plates to juggle in everyday life, be that family, work, goals, finances, relationships, or health, mental chatter has become the norm. I read something recently which summarises my point exactly. "My mind is like an internet browser. There are least 27 tabs open, 8 of them are frozen, and I have no clue where the music is coming from!" Relatable much?

Calming the mental chatter that bombards our minds day in and day out has a profound effect on the quality of our lives, and it is one of the most liberating things we can do for ourselves.

Sometimes, this mental chatter is fine and totally harmless. Other times, it shows up in ways that do not benefit us at all. For example, when it becomes negative self-talk, self-doubt, self-harming inner conflict and thoughts that lean towards I can't do it or I'm not good enough. Or unwanted emotions such as anger, judgement and jealousy. We have all been there.

Therefore, managing and calming your mental chatter, turning the volume down, will cause a real shift in your reality. It is powerful and will allow you to develop a healthy mind which is essential for mental well-being.

The effects go even further than this. It has been proven by research that the health of your mind will affect the physical health throughout the rest of your body. For example, if you suffer from chronic problems, it is likely to be impacted by how you use your mind. Research has proven that thoughts correlate significantly with various symptoms in chronic health conditions.

Many years ago, my goal was to become a serial entrepreneur. After a few failed business attempts I fell into a period of stress, labelling myself as a loser who will never achieve his dreams. I indulged in endless negative self-talk and slowly started to develop digestive and bladder issues.

What was interesting was that doctors couldn't find anything physically wrong with my body to cause such an issue. This was because, physically, I was well. It was my poor mental state that was making me unwell. The stress and pressure I placed on myself, being frustrated over my failed dreams, was taking its toll on my body.

## Bliss is Our True State

My overactive bladder was caused by stress and intense conflict with the other founder of my business startup. I went to see several doctors who diagnosed it as a chronic problem, and I was told that it's likely to never go away. Surgery was suggested to fix the nerve problem, but it was never a true option for me. Another doctor suggested psychological problems. I worked with a range of therapists, including a hypnotherapist, for over 5 years. I felt amazing after each hypnosis session and loved it, but it didn't make any difference with the bladder problem. I started to believe that it was not related to my psyche and that it was physical.

I attended a personal development event in the UK. At some point during the weekend I suddenly felt that I don't have that urge that I usually have. I immediately thought it was related to my emotional state. I had to maintain a euphoric state during the whole event, which was incredible but exhausting.

I tried to manage my mental state in everyday life, but it's pretty obvious that you can't maintain that peak state all the time as it's an unnatural way of living. The positive effect of the weekend on my bladder quickly disappeared and I was continuing to live with my problem but managing during day to day life.

Years later, as my coaching business was taking off, I was researching how to help clients to control their negative thinking. My goal was to find a way to help my clients tame their negative thoughts. I realised that the key was to get out of your head and to truly observe your thoughts as if they are not a part of you.

The further I progressed on the path of becoming a teacher for my clients, the more the quality of my own life improved. Learning about the law of choice and applying it had a massive impact on my happiness, satisfaction and overall well-being. Amazingly, my bladder problems began to disappear. The more I discovered that I am not my thoughts and that I have the power over them, the more my chronic problem disappeared.

## The Notification Center in Your Brain

You can compare your mind to the notification center of your mobile phone. A thought coming into your head is like a notification on your phone. You have the choice to read that email popping up on your phone when you want to. You also have a choice to engage with that thought.

Imagine getting 1000s of notifications on your phone daily and you try to engage with each of them, analyse them, wonder about them etc.

You start listening to a podcast, and then after two minutes an email notification pops up and you start reading the email right away. Immediately another notification comes up from YouTube and you start watching the video as you get another notification from Facebook.

You'd go crazy, wouldn't you?

So why do this with thoughts? Why engage daily with negative thoughts like "I'm not good enough, I can't do it, I'm a loser, it always happens to me, etc."

This behaviour leads to an unhealthy mind and is a sign of poor mental well-being. Just like opening every app every time a notification pops up, engaging on every negative thought coming into your head is a sign of an unhealthy mind.

I am certain you have found strategies to reduce phone dependency such as limiting notifications to important ones. (I don't care that Amazon just dispatched my wife's cucumber face lotion.) It's best to turn off all notifications completely when doing productive tasks such as studying, office work, or spending time with family and friends.

Good mental health is the same as healthy phone usage. You have the freedom to choose which thoughts to engage with.

Thoughts arise at a rapid rate for all of us. There is no way to stop them. You can have a thought in a split second. You can have dozens of thoughts within a handful of seconds.

Unfortunately, you can't turn off the notifications coming into your brain like you can on your phone by putting it on flight mode or do not disturb. There is no permanent solution for that. That's why so many people drink alcohol when they are stressed. It's a way to temporarily numb the mind. Excessive eating and binging TV series also distract your mind.

Our thoughts are just like notifications on our phone, just like clouds in the sky. We look up, see a cloud and it passes by. The next cloud comes and it passes by. When a thought pops into your head, notice it, choose to think it or to let it go like a cloud floating by.

## Being Present is Key

One common question is how being present can help you tame your thoughts. You don't have to become a Buddhist monk and practice mindfulness all day. Rather, use presence to become observant of your thinking and then consciously give dis-empowering thoughts less power. You can sit on a bench in a quiet park or a busy meeting at work, the key is to be present with your thoughts. Let's have a look at the kinds of thoughts we have in order to understand why presence is the key. We can put our thoughts into two sets of categories: positive/negative and past/future.

A worry such as "I'm going to fail the driving test" is a negative future thought. Reminiscing about your amazing trip to Greece last year is a positive thought about the past. Thoughts are usually past or future oriented, but rarely in the present. Even a thought like "what should I do right now?" has a forward tendency as you are concerned about the future outcome of your action.

## Practical Tips for Becoming Present

Understanding that being present is the key, the next step is to get out of your head. This will help you to engage less with your thoughts, especially the dis-empowering ones. The main way to get out of your head is to focus on your body. This includes our basic senses: seeing, hearing, tasting, and touch, but also sensations such as your breath and touch.

Imagine you are in a classroom and you are in a present state. This means you are listening actively to the lecturer without analysing every word. You notice how your small right toe is itchy. This reminds you of how you stepped on a bee during your last holiday. Next, you are thinking how often you are unlucky during holidays and that bad things always happen to you. Half an hour later you are still in your head, engaged in negative self-talk and how unfair the world can be.

How do you get out of your head again? The same way you got in!

Focus on your body. You could focus on your right toe again.

You could also put your attention on your breath, which has the advantage that it's a bodily movement that has to happen every few seconds for you to stay alive. That recurring breath is a great reminder to regularly re-adjust your attention and bring you back when you checked out. If your toe would twitch regularly without fail, this would be an equally great way to get you out!

Because of its never-failing nature, most people choose the breath. Breathing is such a great way that a popular practice like meditation has it as an elemental component.

To become present, you can also use your visual sense to look at art, architecture or nature. Put your full attention on a flower and observe its beauty. It's such a powerful way to help you become present. You can use your auditory senses to become present. Play your favourite tune and focus on the sounds of the different instruments and voices.

To become present you can use any form of body sensation:

- Smell - pay attention to the smell of food without embarking on a mental train journey

- Visual - look at beautiful things without analysing them

- Auditory - listen to some great music without getting carried away

- Taste - chew purposefully and pay close attention to how your food tastes

- Touch - a massage is a lovely way to become present and focus on yourself

- Balance - people rarely get distracted balancing on a rope

The best way to become present is to take a deep breath as it combines multiple senses:

**1)** The smell of the air entering through your nose

**2)** Your body movement (touch) like your belly expanding

**3)** As you can't talk while you breathe in, you pay closer attention to the sounds around you

Also, a deep breath into your belly has a calming effect on your body as it reduces stress levels and normalises your heartbeat. Become present to the moment and enjoy your own company.

# CHAPTER 14

# COURAGE

## By James

My name is James Dand. I am known as the "Empowerment Songwriter;" writing songs with a personal development theme, which help to inspire and motivate people to be more. I am also an international speaker, trainer, and coach who has worked with thousands of people and spoken on stage to large audiences in Europe and the UK.

Having worked as a College and University lecturer and manager for many years, I began to feel increasingly unfulfilled, overworked, stressed, and unhappy. My mindset was full of fears and negative beliefs, which were holding me back from happiness and success, so, I invested thousands of pounds on my own development, receiving training from some of the world's top coaches and trainers.

I learnt and applied self-help techniques to remove the mindset blocks that had been preventing me from fully embracing my passion of music. This provided me with the courage to change my life direction, and pursue my dream of being a songwriter, creating my own business, "Inner Anthem." Since then I've written songs for multi-million-dollar companies, best-selling authors, and international trainers.

Too many people die with their "music" left inside them, so my mission is to empower people to express their gifts and reach their potential.

I'd love to hear from you; please reach out and connect with me at:

www.inneranthem.com

info@inneranthem.com

And on social media as "James Dand" or "Inner Anthem"

# James' Conversation

**Have you ever found yourself asking the question, "How did I end up here?"**

For most of my life, I never really considered myself to be a courageous person. Although I'd never shy away from any challenge on the football pitch and would happily face the fastest bowler in any cricket team, I failed to apply that same level of courage in most other areas of my life. Instead, I placed great value on security and control, and feared most forms of change. Perhaps you can relate to this?

A few years back, I found myself repeatedly asking the same question: "How did I end up here?" On paper, I was successful — a well-paid university lecturer with industry experience and an impressive CV, a Manager of Higher Education, an honest husband and loving father. It was everything I thought I would want.

And yet, there I was at the age of 35, sitting in my small, brick-walled, windowless office at the college I was employed at feeling like I was stuck in a prison cell. There were tears rolling down my cheeks onto my grey suit, and I was aware that anyone could possibly walk through the door at any moment and see me crying. I had about five minutes to get my act together before I was due to teach my next lesson. I was overworked, burnt out, not seeing enough of my family, and regularly having to sit in work meetings. I was thinking: This just isn't me. I'm wasting my life away. I don't want to be doing this anymore.

I knew I needed to make a change. But that was easier said than done, and even then I was confused by what that change should be.

A couple of months later, I was sitting in the back row of a Holistic Lifestyle Coaching course, and upon opening the training manual, I came across a question that ultimately changed my life. It read, "**If you were to die today, would you die knowing that you have lived your life fully?**"

As I stared at the page, it suddenly dawned on me that my life at that time had no real purpose. I hadn't been following my real passion or pursuing my dreams. And why? Because I hadn't had the courage to do so! I'd given in to that little voice in my head that was telling me: You aren't good enough, James. You'll never make it. What will other people think if you try to make a change?

After much internal conflict and debate, later that week, I proclaimed to my wife, "I'm going to step down from my manager's position and reduce my working hours so that I can pursue my passion of songwriting!" This decision required much courage. I was leaving behind a well-paid job, whilst I had a wife and young daughter to support, and a mortgage to pay.

It was a Saturday in May when I informed my parents of my decision. I felt uncomfortable doing so. I was feeling guilty and anxious, but I spoke about my inner feelings and reasons for my decision. To my great relief, they were both supportive and empathetic. I later realized that not everyone was as supportive. Certain close friends and family told me that I was "blinkered," "irresponsible," and "selfish" to give up my job to pursue a dream. This didn't get any easier over the next few months when I was bringing in no money from my new songwriting career.

Through applying courage in my choices and actions, I started to become more self-assured and have greater confidence and belief in myself. Some of those painful conversations helped me to create a stronger, more powerful version of myself, which has helped to enhance several areas of my life. Now, through my roles as an empowerment songwriter, international speaker, and coach, I get to inspire others to act through courage.

I know I am not alone in my example above; wanting more from my life but at times not having the courage to take the right action to get there.

## So, what's your current relationship with courage like? Where could you use more of it, and how do you build it?

At certain times we may find ourselves at a crossroads in life and staying where we are doesn't serve us anymore. We desperately want to make a change but are often daunted by the prospect of doing so.

"What if it goes wrong? What if I'm making a big mistake? I don't know how to do it." Bit by bit, we often end up talking ourselves out of it.

We feel suffocated and give in to those nauseous feelings and horror movie images of how our life could go horribly wrong. It's these thoughts and feelings that can sometimes lead to mental health problems, where the anxiety, pressure and stress build up so much that before we know it, we are suffering from depression or a related health problem.

It takes courage to open up to people, to ask for help, to admit that we're struggling. We often think that vulnerability is a sign of weakness, so we avoid the truth. But when we have the courage to own up to the truth, we have the power to make a change.

Let's take a minute to focus on the positive things that could occur by making a change... What do you specifically want in your life? More money? A career you really care about? To be the best at something? A happy relationship? A sense of fulfilment? To follow your passion? To go on an adventure? Freedom?

Whilst all of these things may be desirable and attainable, they require you to make specific changes. Change in any form takes courage and this is where we often hit a stumbling block.

## We Are Often Scared of Change (and our Brains HATE Change)

The majority of people are fearful of change. It takes bravery to make changes in your life and to grow and develop as a person. The classic 'Hero's Journey', which is the basic format of numerous blockbuster movies, involves the hero making a change from the familiar, to embark upon a journey where they face many challenges along the way, defeating numerous enemies, to finally achieve freedom.

Perhaps you are currently on this journey of self-discovery. If so, it will certainly take courage to achieve what it is you want to achieve, to leave the old and start something new, moving towards your vision of having and becoming something more. It will take courage to be vulnerable and admit that the previous way was ineffective, or to admit that you were wrong. It takes courage to let go of old negative habits, self-imposed limitations, and excuses.

Courage allows you to rise above playing the role of the 'victim', and instead to take personal responsibility for the outcomes of your life. It allows you to become more self-aware and to discover who you really, truly are, and what you are capable of, and, most importantly, it enables you to make the changes that will align you with where you are meant to be.

In her book, "The Top Five Regrets of the Dying," Bronnie Ware, an Australian nurse who spent several years working in palliative care, caring for patients in the last 12 weeks of their lives, identified that two of the top five regrets were linked to a lack of courage, namely:

"I wish I'd had the courage to live a life true to myself, not the life others expected of me"; and "I wish I'd had the courage to express my feelings.

"Life shrinks or expands in proportion to one's courage" (Anais Nin).

Choosing to go against fear is being courageous. The key point is this: Fear can be the killer of your dreams and a source of unhappiness if you choose to give in to it, but when you don't give in to it, fear cannot rule you. "Courage is not the absence of fear, but instead it is the ability to 'act in spite of fear'" (Mark Twain).

Making changes to your life, even for the better, is likely to feel daunting. My first thought when I decided I was going to give up my management job was, "But what if I fail?" I was scared that all my years of work would be wasted if I were to fail, and my wife and family were depending on me. This thought alone nearly stopped me in my tracks from making change. The overwhelming pull of security holding me back. Perhaps this has been your barrier to change, too, that paralyzing fear of failing.

Having courage doesn't mean that you will never fail, but without taking a chance in the first place, how can you ever possibly succeed? Even if you do fail, you will often get another opportunity to succeed by trying again. Successful people see failure as a learning tool; a lesson. They recognise that, in order to succeed, they must first go through several failures, and keep trying until they get it right. This takes courage. Are you prepared to fail and fail again in order to succeed?

This one decision may be the difference between you living the life you want, rather than living a life you don't want.

Brendan Francis suggests, "Many of our fears are tissue paper-thin, and a single courageous step would carry us through them." Choose to take that step!

## Following Your Heart

The origin of the word courage comes from the old French word 'corage', from the Latin word 'Cor', which means 'heart'. So the initial meaning of the word was "to speak one's mind by telling all one's heart". This has important connotations, suggesting that to truly be courageous, you must be coming from your own heart. The courageous act should be in alignment with your own spirit and values, which means that you are acting with integrity. Courage is about taking the right actions according to your heart's desires.

E.E. Cummings stated, "It takes courage to grow up and become who you really are."

John Lancaster Spalding suggested, "The highest courage is to dare to appear to be what one is."

Being true to yourself may mean pursuing your inner passions. Ultimately, it is about being the person who you really are inside; not attempting to be somebody else in order to gain approval or avoid rejection, as I had done for many years myself, but instead it's living your life on your own terms in a way that is most natural to you. This is what I started to do when I chose to follow my heart and pursue my passion for songwriting. It takes courage to express yourself and shine your own light.

Pressure from society, family, and friends may have caused you in the past to make decisions that went against who you really are as a person. This has happened to me on numerous occasions throughout my life. I've chosen to stay quiet, to keep the peace, to not give my own opinions, to not do what I really wanted to do, because I was scared of offending others.

I didn't want to cause an argument. I didn't want to be rejected by people. I didn't believe that I was good enough to live my life on my own terms. I didn't give myself the permission to do so. This led to uncertainty, unhappiness and unfulfillment. It seemed like I wasn't living my own life, but instead, the life of someone else. When this dawned on me, I decided to start to live my life on my own terms.

## Strategies to Increase Courage:

Courage is a choice, and it is always available within you. Therefore, you have to make the choice to use courage whenever you can. In my own life, I've realised that courage is like a muscle, I can choose to make it stronger by using it and pushing it further. The more you apply courage, the more benefits you will gain, the more you will expand your comfort zone, and the greater you will be able to cope with life's challenges and problems. Over time, it gets easier, and it can lead you to more happiness, fulfilment, and freedom.

**1- Awareness**. So, aim to become more aware of where and when you are letting fear rule your life. For example, you may start to realise times when you are not speaking-up, but instead just going with the crowd. When you become aware of this, you have a choice. Without this awareness, all choices will continue to occur unconsciously. Become aware of your ego, and how it wants to keep you small, or wants you to blame other people rather than take responsibility yourself. You can achieve this by acknowledging what stories the negative and critical voice in your head is suggesting to you are true. It may help you to write these things down.

**2- Give yourself permission to be courageous.** You can't change who you were in the past, but you do have a choice as to who you want to be in the present and future. It's often a good idea to start off with small challenges. Consider areas or situations in your life that aren't too daunting, which you could apply courage to. Once you start to do this successfully and notice the positive results and experience the positive feelings, you can progress on to apply courage in other more significant situations and scenarios within your life.

**3- Journal this process (optional).** For example, write down the situations when you apply courage, and identify the positive outcomes that occur. You may also wish to perform this process for previous examples of when you have applied courage throughout your lifetime. Reviewing these situations may allow you to shift your mindset so that you can see the value of acting courageously and start to identify yourself as a courageous person. Remember that courage isn't the absence of fear. Instead, it is choosing to take action despite the fear.

**4- Focus on the future vision of what you want in your life, and who you want to be.** Be aware that overwhelm can often occur when your goal seems too far away, or you have too many things to do. Instead of trying to work out how to achieve every single thing all at once, focus on the next small step that you could take. By applying the courage to take one step at a time, you should eventually reach your destination.

**5- Create a supportive environment around you.** If the people around you frequently apply courage in their own lives, then you are more likely to act courageously yourself, so seek out courageous people, and model them where appropriate.

Reading about courage is not enough. Knowing and understanding courage is not enough. The only way that you will make changes is to decide to use and apply courage consistently throughout your life. You already have this ability within your possession. It's yours, nobody else's. You just have to use it to open enough doors to create the life that you want.

# CHAPTER 15

# DEALING WITH ADVERSITY

## By Allan

My name is Allan Kleynhans and I am a workshop facilitator, and international speaker and a coach. I live in London, although I grew up in South Africa.

My early years witnessing obvious brutality and racist segregation are what initially planted the seed in my mind of becoming someone who would eventually go on to learn how to help people transform their painful past.

I help people to heal, release, and process deep trauma. Transforming my own harrowing experience of PTSD, drug addiction, and destructive patterns are the foundation of my skillset.

Over the past 20 years facilitating workshops all over the world, I have helped thousands of people transform their painful past into something that provides deep insight and wisdom.

My work is also centered on spiritual psychology. I love helping people reconnect with their highest truth and their authentic self. I assist people to process their deepest shame and most painful heartbreak. I love seeing them break through what's been holding them back for years.

If I came face to face with my youngest self, I would tell him to love more and worry less about the opinions of others - that held me back for a long time before I learned to get past it.

I love connecting with people - if you want to connect with me, you can on Instagram, Facebook and LinkedIn using my name.

# Allan's Conversation

Adversity is part of life. Nobody gets out of this life unscathed by some degree of adversity. We are all going to encounter it at some point. When we do, we often don't realise at the time that any good can come of it. In fact, most people believe that there is no possible good that can come of an adversity they're facing, whether that's losing a business, losing a partner, or worse, losing a child.

We get trapped in the darkness of our turmoil and don't realise that, at the same time, this very same adversity will also serve us in the long run, because it always leaves us stronger and wiser and often far humbler than we were beforehand.

Unfortunately, when we are young, most of us are not taught resilience and the benefits of managing adversity effectively, so we spend most of our lives trying to avoid it at all costs without realising that we are also missing out on some of the greatest lessons we can learn.

It's true that most of the most accomplished and influential people of our time faced great adversity. How did they turn it around and leverage their pain to create great success and fulfilment? The simplest answer is that they processed their painful experience in a very different way from most people. Thinking is the hardest work there is – conscious, critical and constructive thinking – because it means we must deeply contemplate our fate and ask better questions to find more empowering answers.

If we are going to continue in life and keep striving for more fulfilment, then we must realise that we have the freedom to choose whether we are empowered by our adversity or not. This kind of conscious and constructive thinking is not common among people.

Amid adversity, when things are going awry, most people find it difficult to see past their immediate crisis or pain and ask themselves what the deeper learning and value might be.

So, then the question becomes, 'does adversity always yield value?' The answer is a resounding 'yes'. There is always deeper learning and value. We all have had painful adversity that has also provided opportunities further down the road. We can all trace our current fortune back to some of our darkest and most painful moments if we look hard enough. Adversity always provides new possibilities and opportunities. It's just a matter of time before you discover them. Whether you do depends completely on your perception of the experience you're having during and after.

"Every adversity, every failure, every heartache carries with it the seed of an equal or greater benefit." The first time I read this line in Napoleon Hill's classic work, Think and Grow Rich, I flat-out refused to believe it. It was July 1988, and I was 21 years of age. I had just returned home from the military after two years of service and I was in a state of shock. I was deployed in Angola for seven months in 1987 and it had severely taken its toll. I was feeling the intense effects of PTSD and constantly having nightmares about what I had experienced. I asked myself, 'How can going to war be of any benefit to me?'

I was reading Hill's book because it had been recommended to me as a source of answers. Although I refused to believe this line when I first read it, I wrote it out on paper and stuck it on the wall in my bedroom, and I contemplated it. What I've come to learn since is that the most powerful lessons are often also the most painful to bear. At some point, we all face adversity and it will either define us or break us.

The writer William Ward once said, "Adversity causes some men to break; others to break records." Sadly, for most people, the first part applies, and their suffering is endless and yet completely unnecessary.

They miss the gift that lies within their adversity. I was in that category for many years and I suffered constantly, but I kept reading, learning and applying what I learned, and things began to change for me in very positive ways.

I began to entertain the idea that perhaps there was a gift in my traumatic experience of war. I began to ask myself how I would be able to use this experience to serve others going forward. This question changed everything. I believe it's by asking this question over and over that has led me to where I am today – serving others through my speaking, training and coaching.

This life would never have happened for me if I had remained trapped in my suffering, asking that question I always asked when I was in pain or when I was stressed: "Why does this always happen to me?" Another question I would always ask when I was stressed or feeling low was, "What is wrong with me?" This presupposes there is something wrong with me, and that was how I felt all the time.

What we don't realise is that we are always processing our experiences and our environments through questions, and if we don't ask the right ones, we always get the wrong answers. So, when we encounter a tragedy, or a traumatic experience, it's imperative that we process the experience effectively to be able to move forward and not get trapped in our own misperceptions. These misperceptions are the root of our suffering. The way to do this is by asking empowering questions that provide empowering answers – we are then empowered to act accordingly in service to ourselves and those who need us.

At times, the adversity we are facing can be extremely painful to bear. Imagine facing the possibility of losing your child. As a father, I know that's the most devastating thing for a parent to ever consider. And yet, I also know people personally who have been able to find peace on the other side of their grief after losing their child. They were able to reach this place of acceptance and peace because they chose to attach an empowering meaning to the experience. This doesn't make the pain any less to bear, but it does mean one doesn't continue to suffer endlessly.

Suffering is always caused when we focus on what we've lost. When we choose to shift our focus to what we can appreciate or what we can be grateful for, it changes how we feel about the situation. This takes practice and it's not easy to do when you've encountered what most would call a devastating loss, but it's crucial if you're going to continue to live in this world and it's crucial if you have other family members who are relying on you to be your best.

One of my best friends lost his daughter to cancer. She was only 5. It was extremely painful for him and all who know and love him. However, by changing the meaning he attached to his experience, he has been able to find joy and happiness again. He is one of the most inspiring people I know. When he speaks of his beautiful daughter, he talks about how he was privileged and blessed to have spent 5 years in the presence of an angel and for that he's eternally grateful.

That takes a tremendous amount of courage.

To keep choosing an empowering meaning when the mind wants you to focus on what you've lost is very tough, but it makes all the difference as to whether you find a reason to continue living a full life or whether you spend the rest of life suffering in bitter despair about everything.

I have another very close friend – we've been friends since we were 8 years old. His son is currently facing a fight with cancer. He's only 15, nearly the same age as my son. They've been friends since they were born. It breaks my heart to know my friend and his family are going through this experience. And I also know that, in some way, they will all have to find some empowering meaning to be able to go on fighting. I've spoken with my friend and his son and I'm inspired by their attitude. The young lad is always smiling and convinced there's a bigger reason for this experience, even though they may not understand what it is now.

My personal belief is that life is a mysterious journey that always provides exactly what we need to fulfill our earthly spiritual curriculum. It's true that most people will never understand this or realise this important aspect of life. Life is the ultimate schooling environment, and, while we are here, we all have lessons to complete and learn. Many of these lessons are extremely painful and we don't know why they occur. It can help to believe that at some point, even if we don't know why now, we will come to understand the bigger lesson and how it applies to our lives.

If we are going to be our very best self while we are alive on this earth, and serve our families and others to the best of our capacity and ability, we must learn to welcome adversity when it occurs and ask ourselves the following questions: "How can I use this experience to grow? What can I learn from this that will allow me to serve others even more powerfully? What else could this mean? What can this experience teach me to be grateful for?"

These are questions that will change your experience of adversity from one of suffering to one of benefit. And, when you benefit, I believe it's your duty to pass on your learning to those you love and those you serve. After all, life is more rewarding when we are adding value to other's lives. What better way to add value than to share the wisdom and insights gained from our darkest and most challenging moments?

One of my favourite things to tell my audience is, "Nothing is ever in the way, everything is always on the way." It's a great reminder that life is a journey and like every journey, there are obstacles and detours along the way and even the occasional dead-end. But that doesn't mean the journey has come to an end – it just means we have to adjust and adapt and continue on as we were before, the only difference being that we have gained experience, knowledge, and wisdom, all of which allow us to navigate the possible obstacles that may lie ahead with more certainty and ability.

This makes life a far richer experience and offers us all the ability to discover more of ourselves in the process. Just as strong trees grow against the strongest winds, people find their greatness when they look for the value in their challenges. We would all do well to remember that life happens for us and not to us – the very next time you encounter adversity of any kind, try saying this to yourself, "This happened for me, not to me!"

Since I was first asked to contribute this chapter to this great work, a lot has changed in my life. I've faced some severe challenges in my business, which some would label as adverse. My best friend of 30 years is fighting for his life in hospital against lymphoma. I pray he makes it through so he can continue to be the great father and husband he is to his family.

In spite of this, I take heart and inspiration from another great man, who inspired millions to rise above their own challenges and keep smiling in the face of adversity – Sean Stephenson, who was born with osteogenesis imperfecta. Sean was only 3 feet tall, had fragile bones and spent most of his time in a wheelchair. Sean was predicted not to live very long after his birth, but he defied logic and created a magnificent life becoming an inspiration to millions of people worldwide.

Sadly Sean recently passed away, aged 40, due to a head injury when his chair fell from a platform. I share this with you here in closing because I want to tell you what Sean said from his hospital bed moments before he took his last breath. He said the same thing he's said many times to many audiences who came from great distances to hear him speak: "This happened FOR me, not to me."

He took nothing for granted. He had an amazing sense of humour and made people laugh and feel good about themselves. He found the joy and blessing in everything including his own condition, and even right at the very end of his life, when he felt himself slipping away, he again said what he truly believed: "This happened FOR me, not to me."

Remember these words well because when you face what seems like an insurmountable problem or an unexpected adversity that brings you to your knees, bringing these words back to mind will help you find your way back from the edge much stronger and better than before.

Stay blessed and make your life a magnificent example of what your soul looks like on fire.

# CHAPTER 16

# SELF ACCEPTANCE

## By Tina

I am a coach and trainer who trained originally as a nurse. I then went into ministry 25 years ago. I have worked with the confused, forgotten, unloved, and discouraged for many years.

I run a Christian retreat centre (open to all), prayer centre and training centre in a beautiful hamlet in Yorkshire, very close to the M1. I love people and am passionate to help them learn how to love and fully value themselves. We become better leaders of ourselves and others when we start with listening to and ourselves as well as others.

If I could chat with my younger self I would coach myself!! I would show myself how to forgive myself quickly, and how to cherish myself. As a younger person I was so very hard on myself and I would show myself in what ways to change, and how to spot myself doing it and cherish myself instead.

Why do I run a retreat centre? Because the world is full of hurting people who hurt people. We all need time, space and support to become our best selves and it starts with learning how to listen to and love ourselves. I suppose I am doing what I would have wished for at many times in my own life - only I didn't know I needed it!

I got into this change in work dramatically after my husband and I decided we wanted a year's break from years of inner city parish ministry. God had other ideas! It's beautiful here and the first six months here restored us physically and emotionally, and we've had the privilege of helping many people here to revive, refresh, and strengthen themselves.

If you would like to connect with me, that would be awesome!

My retreat website
https://www.eaglesriseinternational.com/
My coaching non-profit website
https://transformationisforall.com/
Or email me on TinaCHodges@gmail.com

# Tina's Conversation

If you saw me today, you'd never know I was a victim of childhood abuse. Since then, I have gone through a complete transformation. It's possible. I want you to take heart and have hope.

If you are in that place where you just think everyone would be better off without you, you're wrong. I used to be there too. I no longer believe that. Beliefs change.

In my journey toward healing, I learned to distinguish between mental struggle and reality.

It saved my life.

I once spoke in front of a couple of thousand people on how I went from surviving to thriving. I'd just lost four family members in a year and shared about how I survived death, sexual abuse and marriage betrayal, miscarriages, and trauma, amongst other things.

After I spoke, I was greeted with many who related to my story. To me, that says a lot about how many good people have been trashed by moments in life.

We all wanted to, in the words of Maya Angelou, "thrive, not just survive." That bound us together. I'm expecting you are one of them. You may not have experienced gut-wrenching pain to the extent that I have... or you might have gone through more tragedies than I can even imagine... but it's really not about comparing and measuring scars - it's about sharing victories. Let's find and share the path to overcome our trials.

The three most important things you can listen to in life are yourself, others, and God.

Also, the three most important groups of people you need to be careful listening to are yourself, others and God!

## The Trouble With Listening to Ourselves

I hated myself from a young age. One tragedy after another stole my innocence. I thought nothing could be done about it and that I was damaged forever. I was accidentally knocked into an outdoor swimming pool at the age of three and drowned. When I came to, I was 'vomiting water.' Before then, I had no fear. After that incident, it was my constant companion.

My stepdad grew up in poverty, and was abused and neglected as a child. My Mum was away working most of the time. I got used to having no one to confide in. I struggled with bullies everywhere I went.

Thinking back, it was such chaos it felt like growing up in a war zone.

Babysitting me was a family 'friend', an undiscovered married paedophile, who threatened, coerced and blackmailed me into doing things no child should know about, crossing boundaries. I don't know who I grew to hate more - him or me. With the defilement came thoughts and feelings of self-hatred. I felt dirty. Whilst secure externally, deep down I was ashamed. I could see no way to reclaim my fractured childhood innocence.

We didn't get much help and support in those days.

Financially, spiritually, emotionally, or practically. Our family didn't have any good friends except the paedophile and his wife. Those were the days my brother and I learned to hide from social services because we were left home alone so much. Like many today, it seemed I was trained to live life for others' amusement and pleasure and not for my own self. I became desperate for any kind of affirmation.

I had zero sense of self, which was not good. Looking back now, I see that our internal scripts become warped as we become emotionally and spiritually bruised and battered by life. We are often great recorders but rubbish interpreters. Unless we get the right support to detox toxic thoughts, they become like poisonous lifelong squatters. We can do what we can to drown out the critical rhetoric, but without help, we become permanently impacted by such things: we let their thoughts overwhelm us so we can find no sense of peace.

Accepting lies about ourselves seems often the path of least resistance and the only way out.

## Listening to Others

Our friends and family often become our worst critics.

How many grow up with nothing good said about them? How many grow up with far too few words of encouragement and affirmation? How can we thrive with an absence of 'supporters?' We can't!

I dreaded standing up for myself. But, when I started standing up for myself and cherishing boundaries, good things started to happen. I found out that I was my own biggest critic even before I realized that others could shape my own thoughts on the matter. One day I had it. I decided I didn't have to believe the lies and criticisms that my mind was filled with. My thinking was so crooked that I couldn't actually think or feel in a straight line - talk about obstacles, it was an obstacle course! It had become agony and I gained enough awareness to realise that.

So I put my first ever boundary in with ...myself!

I decided not to listen or take note of any critical voice that was in my head and would instead be led by concrete facts alone and even more, positive facts. I didn't know why they were in my head but I realised that my mind was not my 'friend'. These thoughts would gang up against me and rob me of my peace and self worth.

How can you recognise a toxic thought? Your heart sinks, you become confused, you lose your joy, and you become fearful or angry. So whilst I continued to 'listen' to myself, I stopped 'taking to heart' the toxicity which stole my sense of self worth. Ironic really. But something wonderful happened after that. I realised I couldn't stand it from others either. So I stopped hanging around friends who were critical and hung around people who could see my worth instead.

We're talking years here. It wasn't an overnight improvement. Slowly, by listening to my 'loving' self, I got better. Occasionally I would get overwhelmed by toxic thinking, dreaming of taking my life when I did, but I vowed to myself I would not act on it. And I never did. This is when I also started to listen to my faith. I went to church because the people were nice. It was years before I had any kind of faith though.

## Listening to God

Our opinion of whether God exists may well be shaped by life's circumstances. Many believe that faith in a greater power is a divine joke, when God seemingly allows good people to suffer and does nothing to help. At least, that's what many people who don't believe think. That's what I used to think. I got to see the coincidences between when I was seriously contemplating suicide and the local vicar spotting me though his lounge window and popping out to invite me in for a cup of tea with him and his wife. The coincidence spoke to me. Not God. Not some angel or bright light. But the pattern.

In this day and age, we compartmentalise spirituality into a certain place in our lives and some of us never go there. It's too surreal, too improbable and unprovable. The Jewish concept of wholeness doesn't compartmentalise our well-being like this, but sees faith and spirituality affecting the whole of our lives. I'm not for empty religion or practices. But I am for faith in God (for those who don't believe then let me use the word 'Love' instead). I believe love heals. God's love does anyway.

This isn't a book about faith, but about hope, so I'll leave it there, but feel free to allow your journey in loving yourself to include God, as many people with low self esteem have found their lives transformed when they have included God in their life's journey. That's why today I help many people walk into a place of positive self-esteem and freedom. Because I've been there and because I include faith in my path towards wholeness.

Many people relate to having a low self esteem because of what has happened to them. But we cannot allow our journey to dictate our value. I once spat on a £10 note, screwed it up, rubbed it in my armpit, trod on it, and then asked the group what they thought the note was worth. They all rightly recognised that its worth hadn't changed. What it had been through hadn't changed its worth. We can't see our self worth through our history. Our worth doesn't change because of our journey.

If you don't want to be your own worst enemy then don't be. Instead, get help and be your own best friend. Create experiences and relationships which draw out your value. As my daughter said when I asked her about low self esteem, "I don't think low self esteem can be solved by simply being told something. You need an experience that reaffirms your abilities."

Another friend said, "whatever made you feel like this is not how you were created to be, it's not your final destiny - God can restore your true identity!"

Even if we feel broken we can rebuild our lives and, like broken bones in a body, with the right support, healing can make us stronger than we were before. What we cannot do is thrive when we cannot influence our environment positively. If a nurse uses the wrong dressing on a wound, that dressing can accidentally rip off any new healing when it is changed. In other words, environment matters.

Consistency matters, too. Kind, loving words build up over time. If we're not in an environment filled with kind, loving words, we need to make one by offering that kindness to ourselves. Not only do we believe ourselves more than others, but our own words are more powerful than any words spoken by others.

Remember, our thoughts are the result of our external influences, so when our external factors change for the better, our thoughts slowly follow suit.

Our personalities are as unique as our fingerprints yet education and workplace do not take this into account. That some of us need more reassurance than others is not a bad thing - it is a fact. Whether it's due to our personality or our upbringing is irrelevant. We will thrive if we get what we need.

If I am weak in areas of my life such as social skills, or mathematics, it says nothing of my value. We all have different gifts and abilities, so we need to keep seeking until we find the area that we soar in. If we need a different environment to find that, then so be it.

Individuality is what makes life so interesting and we are such a precious gift to each other. Just remember you are fearfully and wonderfully made next time you look in the mirror. There is no one like you!

# CHAPTER 17

# PERMISSION TO PLAY

## By Emma

I am a clown - (we are the observers of life, think Shakespearian fool or court jester, we never know more than our audience and always come from a place of kindness) who wants to change the world. I am on a mission to get one million adults to play. I play in the world on my podcast Clowning Around, in my theatre shows, keynotes across the world, MCing events and in my upcoming book: Clowning Around: Lessons from a Clown. I also play in the business world with clients including Bloomburg, Barclays, GE and countless brilliant individuals.

I have been drawn into this world of play as it saved me from believing I was not lovable and not enough. I wish that when I was younger I had not been afraid of being all of me, Play has enabled me to have the courage to look at my emotions and trauma and trust that I am and always have been enough. Playing involves exploring who we are, being open to all we can be, being present in the moment and a huge amount of laughter, silliness and joy.

Connect with me: emmastroud.london

instagram: emmastroudldn and
clowningaroundpodcast

email me: hello@emmastroud.london

# Emma's Conversation

Hi, my name is Emma, and there are two things you need to know about me.

First, I'm an accomplished businesswoman.

Second, I'm also a life-long clown. And I mean that literally. Think improvisation. Think Whose Line is it Anyway? Because of my love for improvisation and comedy, I've always appreciated the importance of play in my life. However, as I ran my businesses at certain points I lost the ability to play. I began to feel like I had to put on a mask, I thought if I want to be successful and taken seriously in the business world, then I have to be SERIOUS. And so I realised very quickly that I couldn't tell anybody that I do comedy and definitely couldn't tell them that I'm actually a clown.

*'I'll keep that part of me hidden'*, I decided to myself. I stayed hidden until I turned 37 and after having two businesses fail, I realised that the mask I wore of being somebody that I thought I should be was no longer serving me.

What I have come to realise is that what makes my heart sing is helping others play. Now, Emma, you might be thinking, of course Play is important to you. You do talks. You put yourself on stage on a regular basis. Play is your thing. But me? I don't have time for that. I'm too busy being an adult!

I get where you're coming from. I do.

However, as I have travelled across the world working with an array of people, it has become abundantly clear to me that as adults we NEED to give ourselves the space and the time to play.

## So, what is play? What do I mean?

Play is a state where you are fully present. You are immersed in one thing. You are engaged actively in what you're doing, completely bereft of worry about the outcome. Free of worries. Free of anxieties. Now, if your adult brain is reading this, which I'm assuming it is, you will most likely be saying, I know what play is. I was a child, once, after all. But I don't think that has any relevance in my life or my personal development today. Life as an adult is about achievements, getting things done, not play, your adult brain is saying. I have to pay bills. I have to look after my family. I have to... The list is endless, isn't it?

However, I wonder what difference it would make if you were to take off the ADULT mask and let the child inside you out for a little while. That child hasn't left you. Let the child out for a while and see what happens.

Letting out our inner child is becoming more common in the modern world. Go to any shop and you'll see a huge array of adult colouring books or adult games. (No, not those kinds of games!). Those things sell like hotcakes because they're all designed to help us express ourselves. There's a reason for that. Play helps us to explore, relax, let go of the banal pressures of everyday life; because play is freedom.

Play doesn't simply happen, though. When you're first starting, it has to be planned. It has to be diarised. It's something that you can do by yourself or with others and the more I find time to play the more other things become less important. There are many books written by wise people about the thoughts humans have when they are on their deathbed.

At the end of our lives we don't concentrate on our salary or bank balances. We think about more important things: shared experiences, adventures, moments of togetherness and joy. This is what constitutes play.

Play can be different to everybody, just like when you look at a class of toddlers - some toddlers will be playing with sand, some will be building extraordinary things out of lego that our adult brains can't quite recognise, some toddlers will be painting and exploring different colours and shades with their hands, some will be playing with imaginary friends.

And, just as each toddler plays in a completely different way, so do we. The word Play will evoke different feelings and emotions in every single one of you. The question that I want to pose is: **What keeps you from playing more now?**

When I think about play, I think of that beautiful space of pure enjoyment, that moment when nothing else matters. Being absolutely, positively present and absorbed in what I'm doing.

Just thinking about playing makes me smile!

As I write this, I'm smiling now because, as a clown and performer, I think of my spaces for play, the rehearsal room, or the stage where I do improvisational games. These thoughts take me to a place where I'm doing improvisational games. Those are the games of my life, where I have explored my skills in being present, listening to myself and creating the ability to say yes. (I'll get into saying yes more later.)

When I look back over those skills, skills I've spent years learning and perfecting, and the experience of being in that place of play, that state of play, where I can just play for the sake of play, such memories make my heart sing.

Of course, I'm in no way suggesting to you, dear reader, that you should go out and pursue a career in clowning or comedy.

What I am suggesting is that you find your own way to play. I have travelled the world and worked with many audiences; I have found that regardless of one's job title, background, country of origin or religious values - everyone enjoys letting their inner child free. When people are given a chance to experience play and what it means to them, their whole concept of mental wellbeing changes. A weight is lifted of their shoulders, suddenly, everything is possible - you deserve this feeling.

A lot of people that I have worked with have said "well I'm not creative", of course they are, but at some point, they have been judged for being creative or decided themselves that they are not creative because they are, you know, an adult.

Unfortunately, as we grow up, we often get preoccupied with all the things we need to do as adults. We become a Human Doing, and we forget to be a Human Being.

Play allows us to be in touch with who we really are. Play is freedom. Play is joy.

So, I wonder:

As you reflect upon Play in your life, do you give yourself the time to just Be?

Do you allow yourself the time and space to play? If not, why? I help adults explore what Play is by analyzing the four words I use to beautifully spell the word PLAY. Let's look at each of those four words now and review what they can mean for you.

## P: Permission

So many of us believe that we have to act a certain way. We think we have to be this sensible grown-up and that means being mature and hard-working.

I've worked with some of the most successful humans on the planet, and I can honestly say that every single one of them is still deeply scared.

We all have thoughts that hold us back. People call it their inner critic, the negative voice inside your head. It's the annoying monkey inside our brains clashing the symbols together.

*I don't play. I'm a doctor.*
*I have to be very serious. This is how I am!*
*I can't do that. I'll just look silly.*
*If I suggest that, they'll never give me that promotion.*

Those are the phrases of our inner monkey dialogue. For me, it was: *They'll never take me seriously. They're not going to believe that I can help them. They're just going to dismiss me as someone silly and frivolous.*

For a time, this monkey got so loud in my head that I stopped being Emma. I stopped playing. I honestly believe this is why my first two businesses failed. I was too afraid. I didn't give myself permission to Play.

What do you need to do in order to give yourself permission?

My most vital moment of giving myself permission came when I found myself in a business support group. One aspect of this group was that we often had interesting dress themes and on this particular evening it was a fruit theme.

I decided that rather than wearing something an adult would pick... I would dress as a banana. I was the only banana at the group! (Perhaps this wasn't surprising!)

All the rest of the women wore beautiful fruit-themed attire, they wore elegant pineapple prints and cherry brooches. But as I left at the event dressed as a banana, and as I went around London with the same outfit, I realized that this was what the world needed from me. Everyone needed me to demonstrate giving myself permission to play. That evening, I walked around the city, chatting to people of different ages and backgrounds and opening up their potential for play.

Now, I'm not suggesting you have to dress up as fruit to give yourself permission to play. That was just my journey, how I realized that I had to give myself permission to explore this playful part of myself.

Try this: Close your eyes, take a moment to breathe, and ask yourself how you really want to play? If you could choose any form of play, what would you choose to do?

For some people it's geeking out over Legos, whereas others would rather go and shoot some hoops at a basketball court. Or it might be crafting something from a design you made yourself. We'll all choose to play in a different way because we're all unique, and that's okay!

So my question for you is this: How will you give yourself permission to play?

## L: Love

When we play, we open our hearts. We allow ourselves to access our younger selves.

In this ever-speeding world, there is less and less time for us to breathe and choose how we best want to act. By allowing ourselves to play, we give ourselves the ability to slow down and love ourselves. At the heart of every personal development book or personal growth journey, there is the choice to look at oneself and come to terms with all the parts of who we are.

Some of those are parts we might not like that much. Through play, we can explore these different parts of ourselves. We can slow down. We can be present and focus on just one thing. By doing that, we can clear ourselves and subconsciously open our hearts. It's time for love.

When we come together as humans, whether virtually or in real life, there is a shared connection. When we play, this connection deepens; we allow love to come into our world through play so extraordinary things can change.

During a game or a team sport there is a connection and shared experience between all of those involved. If you're not into sport and your idea of play is sitting and drawing, it is still giving yourself a moment to have a deeper connection with yourself. All of these forms of play, and every other form you can think of all have one important thing in common: **love.**

Those that play allow themselves to love more, to be loved more and are more open and curious. The potential of how much more present they can be in the world.

Who knew that play can have such an impact? If you are blessed to have children in your life you will recognize that they want your time; when you sit and play their games with them, they sense the love that is coming from you by playing with them. So I wonder how playing and giving yourself the permission to play can open your heart to all the love you deserve?

It is brilliant that you are reading this book. I applaud you for your wise choice!

However, I know from experience that I can read a lot of books and think: *Yeah, that makes sense. That could make you happier, and it could be life- changing.*

But then in order to make a substantial change, you have to go beyond thinking. You have to choose to show up in the world and take responsibility. You have to take action. It just so happens that Action is the next word we'll discuss!

**A: Action**

So far in your reading of this chapter, what things have come to your mind? Perhaps you've been thinking, *I would love to do that.* Or, you may have thought, *I wonder if I could still play that game.*

What do you need to do now? **You need to take action.** Otherwise, there is the potential that you could read this book, love what it has to say, maybe even hand it over to someone else because you loved it so much, and yet do nothing yourself!

Go get your diary now!

Schedule time for you to go and play, the sooner the better.

As you make that note in your schedule, there may be a part of you saying, *I can't do this! I'm too busy. I don't have time to play. What do you mean diarize?*

As adults, we are under many pressures, both real and imagined. We live in a time-poor society, but I don't buy into that anymore, and you don't have to either.

I believe that we can create whatever time we need by taking action and putting in the things that we want to happen in our lives, into our diaries. Put play as part of your next week, be it half an hour where you go play with your kids, go swimming or hang out with your friends and have a laugh.

From my own experience, I also think it really helps to do this type of thing with other people. My group of fellow clowns and I do something together every couple of weeks. We call it our play time, where we will get together with the sole intention of playing. Now, I have to be brutally honest here. Sometimes, I look at my diary and think, *I don't have time for that. I've got to get on.*

However, because I've made a commitment to other people and to myself, and because I love myself, I turn up.

It's only two hours of my week! I do have time for that! (I can certainly find two hours to scroll through social media every week! I can find two hours to procrastinate and watch some box sets.)

When I do get there and start to play, when I let go of all the adult constraints, when I take action because I showed up, I feel brilliant. I feel like everything has opened up again. I feel like I've given myself permission to love myself.

I've learned a powerful lesson; because I take action and make time for play, something changes about all the other adult-things in my life, things I'm constantly concerned about and challenged with. These challenges don't go away of course, but they do feel different after play.

Try it!

Put play in the diary. Get a group together and try playing together. Chat with other people, or create something new. Whatever play looks like for you, even if it is as simple as playing with your child and vowing not to pick up the phone for a few minutes. Even if you just take some time to forget about all the washing that has to be done. When you take action, when you prioritize it, how might you feel afterward?

Now, I make a livelihood out of playing, but even someone like me can feel the challenge of making sure they do this on a regular basis. That's why I'm asking you to take action and then notice how you feel from the experience. I'm guessing you'll feel amazing! Feel the love because you're giving yourself permission to play!

## Y: Yes

The Y in play is extremely important.

We improvisers, people who prefer to create with no script, are usually good at thinking on our feet. But you know what? The irony of it all is that we have to work to be good at improvising. Like anything else, it is a skill that needs to be developed. Improvisation is not just winging it. In fact, if you try to improvise in a business setting when you don't have any knowledge or experience you're likely to flounder.

There's no fun in that at all.

When I give talks about improvisation and why it's important for me, I like to talk about how improvisation is a set of skills. You all have skills that you have developed over time, whether you are an accountant, a lawyer, or a teacher, a mother, or an activist. As an improviser, I've spent the majority of my career exploring and playing with improvisation.

When we play, we allow ourselves to go into different worlds. Sadly, as adults, this world of play is generally quite hidden. By creating a mindset of yes and, it's quite extraordinary to see what doors start to open.

I'm sure you've all had moments where you had a brilliant idea. You go and share that idea with someone, and they use the phrase, *"yeah, but..."*

Have you ever been that person yourself? Were you the person that said *"yes but"* to someone else? I've been in that situation as well, but that is not a side of myself that I want to cultivate!

If you are curious about how you can grow and improve yourself and how you are showing up in the world, how can you cultivate a mindset of *yes and?*

There was someone that I worked with some time ago who, for some reason, whenever they would walk into the room, I would go straight into the *yes but* mindset. There was just something about this person that caused me to not meet them with joy or love. I stopped being creative when I was around them. I thought that maybe I just didn't like them very much! Then, I was challenged by my coach about this particular individual, and I realized that the problem was with my own attitude.

I had developed a real *yes but* attitude when around this person, and they were responding to me in kind.

If you are the one coming up with new ideas, and someone is always putting you down or refusing to hear your ideas, then, of course, the two of you as human beings probably aren't going to get on! From experience, most of us have at least one person that we have this response to.

With the support of my coach, I realized that, by changing my mindset and having a real *yes and* attitude, as well as a *yes how* attitude, something could change about our relationship.

## Yes And / Yes How / Yes But

Having a *yes how* attitude means that you are open to hearing new things. But it does not mean that you are just accepting anything anybody says; you are also asking them to do a bit of the work for you!

Once I had changed my mindset, I walked into a meeting with this individual with a *yes how* and a *yes and* attitude. Almost immediately, our relationship changed. It shifted in a way that really surprised me. But looking back, it shouldn't have surprised me because, at the heart of any improvising is a *yes and* attitude.

It's the idea of accepting whatever someone else gives you and then building on that gift that they've given you. Thinking about play, time to start letting go of the *"no, I don't do that"* or the *"no, that's not how I behave,"* way of thinking. Open your mindset with a curiosity which starts with the simple word that is YES.

This means you have to struggle with your own inner monkey, that inner dialogue that likes to block your own ideas.

If you're not careful, you can start to block your own wisdom.

But I wonder what would happen for you if you instead opted with a *yes and* attitude first to yourself.

What would happen if you said YES to Play?

What if you said yes to the fun, the silly, the off-the-wall, or the bonkers things that make your heart sing? The things that, if you take a moment just to think really about them you would say to yourself YES - I'd love to do that!

Maybe for you that means going on a roller coaster or abseiling through the trees. Or, it might just be sitting and thinking. Whatever it may be, allow yourself time to say yes to play. I have witnessed too many people across too many industries and in too many different countries struggle with the idea of happiness.

When I ask people if they are happy, they turn away and look uncomfortable. This is because I ask them the question with a sense of hope that they are. But, sadly, because of the way society is, we often move away from the things that make our hearts sing.

Now, I appreciate, as I write this, that you, dear reader, will see me as different from you. You may see me as on a different path. You may reason that I can play because I'm writing this and I perform and I create professionally as a clown. But I am no different from anybody else. I merely took some time to realize and remember that things like playing and having fun are at the heart of all of us as humans.

I think it's truly sad that we do not allow ourselves time to do the fun things. Somehow, society has got into a place where we are consumed with busyness and achievement. We moved away from our hearts, the place which is love.

So, I ask you, what if you give yourself some PERMISSION to play, if you give yourself permission to LOVE, if you take ACTION, wanting more play, to have the desire to say YES to more things?

I wonder if that adult mask that you have on fits quite so tightly. I wonder if suddenly other doors might appear for you. I wonder if you could give yourself that gift. I wonder if you now know you deserve to PLAY.

# ACKNOWLEDGEMENTS

We cannot thank enough, each and every one of the authors who have contributed to this project. Without them none of this would be possible.

We are in awe of them and their inspiring journeys. We are honoured to have them in this book, sharing their stories, so openly and generously with the genuine desire to help everyone whose hands this book falls into. We unreservedly admire their dedication to be vulnerable in the pursuit of connecting with other people who could benefit from their message.

Hours and hours and months and months of writing went into this book, and we will forever be grateful to the authors for their contribution.

To the contributing authors, thank you so much for sharing your light.

Jamie and Raeesa

Printed in Great Britain
by Amazon